Contents

Clowning about with Barry Cowan in the 'Day by Day' studio.

2BE or not 2BE

I have always preferred live broadcasting to making recordings. There is of course the risk that things can go wrong unexpectedly, and there is not much you can do about it except keep going. And I suspect that people actually enjoy hearing those awkward moments. At least they do sometimes. In the very earliest days of radio it was all live.

Mind you, the listeners didn't always like what they heard. There's an example of this which dates back to the Twenties when someone wrote to the BBC in Belfast, 'I see from the papers that there is a large increase in the sales of radio sets. This does not surprise me. After last night's programme I am selling mine too!' And the late Charlie Freer once told me that shortly after he joined the BBC, feeling very proud of his new position, he went back to his native West of Ireland and met a local farmer. He introduced himself and asked the farmer if he had heard any of his programmes from Belfast. The reply he got was: 'Ah have, but ah haven't heerd anythin' yet that wud make me lave aff cuttin' turf!'

There's another story I've often heard, so it must be true, that during a live broadcast of a concert from the Ulster Hall, the orchestra was playing a major symphonic work which built up to an enormous climax and then suddenly stopped. At that moment, in what should have been a dramatic pause, a voice rang out from the middle of the audience: 'Do you? We usually fry ours!' Let that be a warning to you, never carry on a conversation in the

BELFAST'S FIRST RADIO.

MUSICAL PROGRAMME

VERY FINE.

MRS. SEEDS' GREAT SUCCESS

CAT ENJOYS A CIGAR-BOX SET.

Last evening the inaugural programme at the new Belfast Broadcasting Station was listened to by thousands as far away as Dublin. The results were generally very good. The musical director, Mr. E. Godfrey Brown, is to be congratulated on an excellent programme as far as choice of music and musicians was concerned. And the operators broadcasted the music very efficiently.

Opinions, here and there and everywhere, agree that the programme was really fine. Mrs. Seeds's songs came through with musical effect, and the glorious voice recorded well in music that had artistic charm and excellence. The Queen's Island Choir did not record so ideally well; the very soft passages were too soft, and disappeared at times, but the full tones were good.

The orchestra was capital, and had the usual defects in recording that all orchestras suffer from—the deeper toned instruments were not heard well, but the upper tones came through pretty satisfactorily. Most satisfactory of all was the fine speech by Earl Haig on behalf of the British Legion. Every word in that beautifully enunciated, fluent and gracious speech was heard distinctly. So was the announcer, Mr. W. Montagu-Douglas-Scott. Mr. Godfrey Brown made a few remarks which were also heard clearly. He has the right kind of voice and diction to carry well.

From Whitehead, Ballyholme and other outlying districts good reports come in. Regarding hearing Glasgow and other cross-Channel stations while Belfast was operating, the fears of listeners-in were unfortunately justified—those who tried found Glasgow a wipe-out, and the others dim in proportion to the nearness of their wave length to that of Belfast. The best of the bunch was the high-power Chelmsford station on sets with the requisite adjustments.

EXPERIENCES ON WIRELESS.

Wireless enthusiasts in Newtownards were all tuned in to Belfast on Monday evening for the reception of the first programme from Belfast Broadcasting Station, and on the whole the results were exceptionally good. One owner of a crystal set was very fortunate and had the programme in its entirety without interruption. A popular item here was that of the Queen's Island Male Choir, which was extremely good, the various parts of the choir being beautifully blended.

A visitor to Donaghadee writes:—While walking towards the pier about 8-30 on Monday evening I received a bit of a shock to hear the strains of Becker's "Little Church" from a loud speaker, and suddenly recollected that it was one of the first items of the opening programme in connection with broadcasting from Belfast. At once interested in the Queen's Island Male Choir, I halted and heard the piece in its entirety; and my first feelings were those of disappointment. This was primarily due to the difficulty of picking up the words—although I know the piece by heart—which would suggest that performers will have to pay particular attention to this important matter, even to the point of over-pronunciation. It is a remarkable difference listening-in and hearing the choir on a concert platform; for whereas on the latter the choir has a beautiful blend and is carefully balanced, there seemed an overplus of top tenor on the wireless, due no doubt to the better carrying capacity of the lighter voice.

A CAT LISTENS IN.

Not the least novel of the many wireless sets used in Belfast last night was one made from two cigar boxes. Even a cat listened in, and when the earphones were placed to her ears the cat purred with pleasure, being obviously tickled with the orchestral tunes.

A crowd of 200 assembled outside the residence of Mr. Nelson, Bloomfield Road, last night, and were delighted with the wireless programme. The singing transmitted through Mr. Nelson's instrument could be heard for a considerable distance up the road, and the various concert items were warmly applauded by the populace. One gentleman in bed in a house nearby heard the programme distinctly.

The pianos used at Belfast station are two Chappell instruments supplied by Messrs. James Vincent & Sons, Great Victoria Street, Belfast.

middle of a concert.

I often envy those who worked in broadcasting at the very beginning, the pioneers of radio. It is interesting to recall that in its very earliest days it was a very informal business. Then for a long while the informality vanished. Now in some ways it has gone full circle. When television came along, there were those who might have written off radio as having outlived its usefulness. I for one am very glad that radio, far from dying off, is alive and well and living in the Eighties.

In Northern Ireland it is now nearly sixty years since the BBC's first radio station came on the air. 2 BE, as the Belfast station was called, should have begun at 7.00 p.m. on the evening of 15 September 1924. Unfortunately there was, to use one of radio's familiar phrases, a technical hitch. But some thirty minutes later the problem was resolved and a young announcer stepped up to the microphone and opened the service with the words: 'This is 2 BE calling.' For the next hour and a half listeners in the Belfast area were able to hear a concert provided by a number of well-known local artists, and with the 'Augmented Station Orchestra' under its conductor, Mr E. Godfrey Brown. As most listeners only had crystal sets, reception was difficult outside the immediate area of Belfast, but there were some who had the more sophisticated and new-fangled valve sets, and with the aid of these, 2 BE's programmes could be picked up in many parts of Ireland.

Tyrone Guthrie, who had just come down from Oxford, was the announcer on that first evening. He was to be one of the first to realise the enormous potential of this new medium of communication. A few years later his radio play *The Flowers Are Not For You To Pick* was a significant success, and a major influence on later writers for radio. But at the age of twenty-three he must have wondered just what he had let himself in for. The original studio was set up in a converted warehouse in Linenhall Street. Before the station opened, microphone tests proved that the acoustics were unsatisfactory. The studio

When 2 BE Belfast opened in September 1924 the transmitting aerials were slung between the twin chimneys of the Albertbridge Road power-station which, in one of its attics, also housed the transmitter Control Room.

sounded like a cathedral and steps had to be taken to deaden the echo. This was done by hanging a dozen sheets in front of the walls – double-bed size and the best Irish linen. Unfortunately this gave the studio the appearance of a mortuary, which probably did little to calm the nerves of first-time broadcasters. Later the sheets were replaced by thick heavy pleats of curtain material, and later still by sound-absorbing panels made of compressed seaweed.

It can't have been easy working in such conditions. The engineers sat in a control room next door and could see into the studio by means of a small observation window. But unlike today they had no means of communicating with those in the studio so there were two large electric signs which ordered the announcer and artists to 'Move nearer the microphone' or to 'Move back from the microphone'. Nowadays a little voice in your ear can give you this kind of information, and sometimes a lot more too!

When not originating programmes from the Linenhall studio, 2 BE relayed programmes from Savoy Hill in London by landline. Unfortunately the line wasn't very reliable and on some occasions nothing materialised for an entire evening. When this happened ad-hoc programmes were organised on the spur of the moment, The long-suffering members of the station orchestra were issued with crystal sets, and had to tune in at 7 o'clock each evening in case they were needed. As a further safeguard the cinemas in the centre of Belfast had slides which could be superimposed over the films they were showing, asking members of the BBC orchestra to go to the studio at once. But on one occasion when a small group of musicians had been filling in to cover a break in the programme from London, they eventually played themselves to a standstill and could play no more. But still the station orchestra hadn't appeared. So an announcement was made inviting 'anyone with talent' to come to the studio. Within minutes there was a queue at the door, and after instant auditions had been held, a

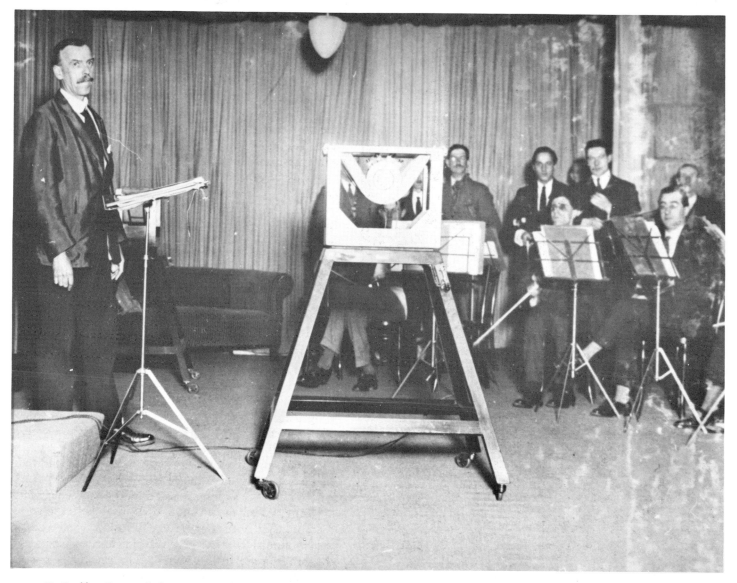

E. Godfrey Brown (left), Director of Music, with a section of the 'Belfast Wireless Station Orchestra', back in 1924. Note the very early 'meat safe' microphone.

I'm just a besom-man by trade,
  I haven't much of sundry brass,
And folk remark in passing by—
  "Mulcaghey isn't in our class!"

At early morn the cuddy's yoked,
  Before the lazy folks get round,
For hills where purple heather blooms,
  Mulcaghey and his ass are bound.

And from the hedges on my way,
  I cut the briars for my trade,
While's contemplate the lovely things
  With which the earth is overlaid.

The dewdrops glistens on the blade,
  The cobweb scintilates with rime,
The joyous chorus of the birds
  Goes up in melody sublime.

At length I reach my harvest field,
  Where busy bees delight to roam,
The load is cut, the cart is filled,
  And "Ned" and I return home.

And now the briars I must strip,
  Prepare the pegs and point the shaft,
All day you'll see me at my work,
  The missus helping at the craft.

*'The Tyrone Constitution' ran a regular column
in which Matt Mulcahy recorded, in rhyme,
'deeds great and small'. The extract above
comes from 'Flower Beggars' in a collection,
'The Rhymes of a Besom Man', which they
published in 1929.*

lengthy amateur variety programme was on the air.

There have been many landmarks in broadcasting in the Province since those pioneering days. On the technical side there was the opening of the high-power transmitting station at Lisnagarvey on 26 March 1936. The original studio in Linenhall Street and the others which had joined it there became redundant in May 1941, when the staff moved into the splendid new Broadcasting House in Ormeau Avenue, the biggest and best studio complex outside London. Unfortunately because of the war it, like many other studios, had to wait until peacetime to have the acoustic treatment completed. On the programme side there were many much-loved characters who made their appearance at the microphone, like Mrs Rooney of Belfast. She survived for twenty years. Matt Mulcahy, the 'Oul' Besom Man from Tyrone' made his debut on 16 March 1927 and continued to entertain Ulster listeners for twenty-five years.

And of course there was *The McCooeys*. As soon as the strains of 'My Aunt Jane' (the signature tune) floated from the loudspeakers of thousands of radios all over the Province the streets of our towns and villages suddenly emptied. The programme rapidly became compulsive listening each week as a wee family grocer called Bobby Greer related the everyday happenings of his friends, the McCooeys. It was the most popular radio serial ever broadcast from Belfast. And its author, Joseph Tomelty, had another huge success the following year when his play *All Souls' Night* received an ovation after its national broadcast in Saturday Night Theatre. James Young had a big success too as Derek the window-cleaner in *The McCooeys*, and this led to his own first radio series, *The Young Idea*, in 1952.

As a youngster I listened to the radio a great deal. I can't remember now whether I decided that I wanted to work in broadcasting because I listened in so much or whether it was the other way round. What I can remember very clearly is that from about the age of ten or

The McCooeys

BELFAST'S RADIO FAMILY CREATED BY JOSEPH TOMELTY

NO. 1. Money from America!

My name's Bobby Greer. I'm a wee family grocer and each week I will be keeping you informed of the everyday happenings of my friends the McCooeys. Many readers will need no introduction to the McCooeys, but for those that do they are a typical Belfast family. Mrs. Maggie McCooey has two daughters Sally and Meta, and a son Willie. Her husband Sammy works in the 'yard and Sarah Blake, her unmarried sister, practically lives in the house.

Sammy's father Granda is a real character. He lives with his son and is friend and counsellor to all. He's a good mate of mine too.

SARAH— LORD, THAT'S A NIGHT TO SKIN A FAIRY GRANDA'S SURE TO GET A FOUNDER IN THAT WATCHMAN'S HUT I WISH HE DIDN'T HAVE TO WORK, BUT THAT RAILWAY PENSION BARELY LETS HIM LIVE.

MAGGIE— THAT MEDICAL BOOK OF YOURS IS FILLING YOUR HEAD WITH FEARS SARAH. IF I KNOW THE OLD FELLA HE IS TAKING GOOD CARE OF HIMSELF!

SAMMY— THAT'S A BRAVE LOOKING CUP OF TEA MAGGIE NOT A BAD PIECE OF STEAK TOO, BUT I WISH WILLIE WOULD HURRY BACK FROM BOBBY GREER'S WITH THE H.P. SAUCE.

SARAH— THAT'S YOUR SAMMY HOME NOW. HE MUST HAVE GOT AN EARLY BUS FROM THE 'YARD

SALLY— FATHER. DO WE HAVE ANY RELATIVES IN THE STATES?

SALLY— THERE WAS A LAWYER IN THE OFFICE TO-DAY AND HE WAS ENQUIRING AFTER THE RELATIVES OF AN AMERICAN MILLIONAIRE SENATOR WILLIAM McCOOEY OF OHIO.

MAGGIE— AH THERE YOU ARE WILLIE, RUN DOWN TO THE WEE HUT. AND GET YOUR GRANDA.

WILLIE— AH MOTHER MY TEA'S GETTING COLD!

I'LL KEEP IT WARM IN THE OVEN. RUN ON NOW I WOULDN'T SLEEP A WINK THE NIGHT IF I DON'T KNOW THE RIGHT WAY OF THIS!

SAMMY— GRANDA HAD AN UNCLE WHO EMIGRATED TO AMERICA IN 1910. WE HAVN'T HEARD FROM HIM FOR A LONG TIME, BUT THAT COULD HAVE BEEN HIM

NEXT WEEK— GRANDA GIVES AWAY HIS MILLION.

NOVEMBER 20, 1964 CITYWEEK 7

THE 100TH EDITION OF 'THE McCOOEYS' The story of a Belfast family Written by JOSEPH TOMELTY Produced by SAM DENTON AT 7.25

From the 'Radio Times', 11 April 1952.

The now defunct 'Cityweek' newspaper regularly devoted a whole page to the doings of the McCooeys.

7

eleven all I wanted for my birthday or at Christmas were things like microphones, amplifiers, loudspeakers, turntables or records. By a happy coincidence this was just after the end of the war and there was a great deal of unwanted communications equipment on the market, so I often got what I wanted. This led to a rather unhappy time for my parents, sister and three brothers, because the house was usually festooned in electric wiring and cables, while I carried out strange experiments in 'broadcasting' from one place to another. The wiring extended through several neighbouring gardens at one time with the kind co-operation of the neighbours, so that a school friend, Ian White, and I could talk to each other from our respective houses. Our microphones bore some famous initials, CBS, but in our case they referred to the Cabinhill Broadcasting System.

Having been born in the mid Thirties I am obviously far too young to remember at first hand the golden days of radio, but for some reason I have always had a deep fascination for the early days. I love reading about them, I love hearing recordings from those times, and in fact I'm sure it must be this which has given me my love of jazz, and in particular the invigorating music of the swinging Thirties.

My first broadcast proper, with the BBC that is, was at the age of eleven. Like thousands of young boys and girls from all over the Province, I wrote to Cicely Mathews and said, 'I want to be an actor.' Appearing in a live radio play lasting all of twelve minutes or so could well have been a traumatic experience, and not just for myself. But I was encouraged to try for auditions with the BBC's Features and Drama departments. Some small parts followed and it was a big thrill to stand in the studio at the end of a live broadcast and hear Maurice Shillington or Duncan Hearle announce to the world: 'And the part of Freddy was played by Walter Love.' The fact that all that Freddy said was, 'Excuse me, sir, there's a man to see you' or 'Look out, here comes the master' didn't seem very important.

I wasn't the only one surrounded by tangles of cable and wire — outside broadcasting in the early days was a complicated business, requiring ingenuity and resourcefulness, as these photographs show. Above: recording a nature study programme; opposite page: the 'Ulster Mirror' team heading for the Marble Arch caves in Fermanagh for a talk on geology.

9

To be a Studio Manager in 1959 required considerable dexterity in playing recorded sound effects for live drama and features. Individual sounds were often 'mixed' into complicated sequences.

Before I left school I had made up my mind that I wanted to have a career in broadcasting. But my parents persuaded me that I'd be better to follow in the footsteps of some of my relations who were accountants. For six long years I did my best. Perhaps it was an inability to count, or because I failed to get through the Intermediate Exam five times, but eventually I got the message across that it was time I did what I had always wanted to do. Still I suppose that as an accountant I can regard myself as an unqualified success! In 1958 the BBC was looking for trainee studio managers. I'm not sure if I knew what a studio manager was. I think someone told me that I would not be a producer and I wouldn't be an engineer, but somewhere between the two.

I applied for the job and to my amazement was accepted. I really was surprised because at my interview I was asked two technical questions and managed to give incorrect answers to both of them. Perhaps the members of the interviewing panel didn't know the answers either! And my new career got off to a bad start when, fresh out of training school, I turned the first programme they let me loose on into a shambles. Presumably nobody was listening because I survived that day, and a few others that followed it.

The point I made earlier about the risk of things going wrong unexpectedly is a very valid one. And sometimes these difficulties can sneak up on you in the simplest of ways. I can remember on *Day by Day* not so very long ago playing a lovely choral version of the song 'My Way' for a nice old man on his 82nd birthday. Unfortunately the opening words of the song go: 'And now the end is near'! Or there was the day when we heard sadly of the death of Gracie Fields and felt that at the end of the programme it would be appropriate to pay a brief tribute to her. We found an album of some of her most famous songs and, without hearing it in advance because there wasn't time, I played the beginning of the record 'Sally' which was perhaps her most famous song of all. But I hadn't realised that it was a medley of songs, and within thirty seconds the music changed to 'Sing As We Go'. I suppose it could have been worse, it might have been 'Wish Me Luck As You Wave Me Goodbye'! I felt very foolish but as someone said to me afterwards, I think Gracie would have enjoyed that.

Searching my memory I can remember the time one announcer, who shall be nameless, slept in. He lived in digs not very far from Broadcasting House and was rudely awakened by an irate engineer who told him he had ten minutes to get to the studio to read the early morning news. He asked the engineer to get someone in the newsroom to phone the Met Office and take down the weather for him. He then grabbed his dressing-gown, leapt into his car and drove very fast down the Ormeau Road. As it was very early and there were no traffic hold-ups he arrived in the studio with seconds to spare and went straight into the studio to read the news. The news editor came in with the weather forecast and during the newsread handed it to him. It was all in shorthand! Or there was a reporter once who took down the details of a big fishing contest in the West of Ireland from the winner who was a Bangor man and who thought the BBC would like to know. But the reporter's pencil was blunt, and when he tried to read it back sometime later, couldn't make out whether the man had caught a mullet in Belturbet or a turbot in Belmullet!

We've had one or two moments of sly humour on *Day by Day*, especially on one of my favourite days — April 1st. 'Clarence McMenamin', a very famous duck-breeder from Ahoghill, made his first broadcast on that day one year. In a number of subsequent programmes Clarence amazed the Ulster public with news of his expertise in breeding such things as experimental three-legged ducks in the Isle of Man, designed to improve the stability of the duck in the winter gales which sweep the British Isles. Perhaps the peak of his success came when one of his prize-winners, a Glory of Galgorm, was chosen by Walt

MUSIC AT NIGHT

Seamus McGoldrick (Violin)
Wilberforce Twomey (Cello)
Havelock Nelson (Piano)

TRANSMISSION: SUNDAY 11th APRIL 1971: 11.21 - 11.45 NI R4 & BASIC
PRE-RECORDED: THURSDAY 1st APRIL 1971:10.30 - 12.00 noon.
RECORDING No: TBE 13/UB943U

ANNOUNCER: And now 'Music at Night' from Belfast. Tonight's
               recital is given by Seamus McGoldrick (Violin)
               Wilberforce Twomey (Cello) and Havelock Nelson
               (Piano). The main work they are to play is the
               song-cycle "Znadi cro Sliczowy" by the contemporary
               Polish composer Ilytch Pielcek. Pielcek was born
               in Breslaw in 1906 and studied for a number of years
               at the University of Czerny. There he was influenced
               by the Finnish composer Gyorgy von Pauk, who had
               devoted himself to the compilation of little-known
               Polish Folk Airs. "Znadi cro Sliczowy" is a set of
               these airs, arranged for Violin, Cello and Piano.
               First Wizic - The Cuckoo.

                    Hark to that rapturous sound so distant heard.
                    Cuckoo! Be still you other creatures all around.
                    Spring is here. Cuckoo!

               WIZIC   pub. Drobny Press.
               Pielcek.
ANNOUNCER: Next, "Zielpic cro Cwizt" - The Maiden's lament in the
               pine forest.

                    Oh slender pine, so tall and yet so strong
                    Tell me when my true love will return.
                    Tell me now, oh slender pine.

               ZIELPIC CRO CWIZT   pub. Drobny Press.
               Pielcek.

                                                    NOUNCER:

BBC announcers sometimes have to cope with
some real tongue-twisters, like this 'script' given
to one unfortunate to read.

12

ANNOUNCER: -2-
               And last in the song-cycle "Znadi cro Sliczowy,"
               Stentlicz im Zlimy - The Game-keeper's Reverie.

                    The flowers are blooming, nature leaps unbounded
                    The maidens in the meadow seem so gay.
                    Oh happy time, why should my heart be sad?
                    Soon Gerda will be here to lie by my side.
ANNOUNCER: STENTLICZ IM ZLIMY   pub. Drobny Press.
               Pielcek.
               That was the song-cycle "Znadi cro Sliczowy" by the
               contemporary Polish composer Ilytch Pielcek.
               To end this evening's recital from our Belfast
               studios, Seamus McGoldrick (Violin) Wilberforce
               Twomey (Cello) and Havelock Nelson (Piano) are going
               to play Schubert's "Zwei Grosscheidt Konzertstucke"
               in B flat major.   The final period of Schubert's
               life was the most prolific, and this work was
               completed only two days before he died from complete
               exhaustion. The score bears a dedication to the
               composer's life-long friend Hans Hocht.
               Zwei Grosscheidt Konzertstucke, by Schubert.
               ZWEI GROSSCHEIDT KONZERTSTUCKE   pub. Mills Music.
               Schubert.
               That performance of Zwei Grosscheidt Konzertstucke
               by Schubert brings to an end "Music at Night" which
               was played in our Belfast Studios by Seamus
               McGoldrick (Violin) Wilberforce Twomey (Cello) and
               Havelock Nelson (Piano).

Disney Studios to play one of the main parts in a space extravaganza called Duck Wars!

And April 1st has proved to be an excellent day for finding highly intelligent competitors for our daily quiz. Even more so than usual. It's not everyone who could rattle off with only a second's hesitation the name of the first British Scientist to win a Noble prize for Chemistry, or tell you straight off that the highest ski resort in the world is at Chactaltaya in Bolivia. But 'William McBratney' from Cloughey, alias Paddy Murphy from the Sports Council, was able to do it.

There are times when the listener remains blissfully unaware of some of the antics 'backstage'. Once an expert on theatre make-up came on the programme and demonstrated his art by making me up with the face of a clown. As I had no opportunity of cleaning it off until the end of the broadcast, the rest of that morning's studio guests had not only to cope with the usual nervousness induced by the microphone – they also had to pretend to be casual in the face of this rather oddly colourful interviewer. Veteran broadcaster Barry Cowan, pictured with me that day on the cover, sailed through this test with full marks.

I enjoy the occasional practical joke, especially if I am playing it. A few years ago Denis Jones joined the BBC in Belfast as an announcer. Rather unkindly I wrote an authentic-looking script of announcements for a recital of Polish songs. When Denis arrived to record the announcements he was told that the Pronunciation Unit had already been consulted and they were unable to give any guidance on how to pronounce some of the extremely difficult words in the script. My heart went out to him as he struggled manfully with the most unbelievable text which included such abominations as: 'Zielpic cro Cwizt', 'Znadi cro Sliczowy', and 'Stentlicz im Zlimy', 'The Gamekeeper's Reverie'. Denis came through what

'Day by Day' celebrated its Fourth Birthday on Monday 8 November 1982. To mark the happy event 'Radio Times' published this cartoon of Walter Love by John Minnion.

must have been a horrendous thirty minutes in the studio with flying colours, and in that sense the laugh was on me. The session was actually recorded and to his great credit he even allowed me to broadcast part of it on a later occasion. I have always had the greatest respect for his sportsmanship.

As I said at the start, there's nothing to beat 'live' radio. And Day by Day is always live. Just as all those who worked in radio in the old days had a lot of fun in doing what they did, so too do we on Radio Ulster in 1982. In Day by Day we like to look at the happier side of life and we enjoy having a bit of crack. In the pages of this book many of my favourite guests share some of their own personal reminiscences of our not-so-long-gone past.

Roy Irvine

The first ten years of Roy Irvine's life must have given him a detailed knowledge of the Province. He was born in Newtownards, learned to walk in Carrickmore, was a junior pupil in both Waringstown and Ballynahinch, and arrived in Belfast at the age of ten. His career spans forty years in the telecommunications business, first in engineering, then later in public relations. While still a teenager Roy started to collect gramophone records and today is the proud possessor of a huge and impressive collection. As well as around 4,000 LPs he still has several thousand old-fashioned 78s, presumably most of them often played and well worn by now, plus a couple of vintage wind-up gramophones and a crystal set. Roy's special area of musical interest centres on jazz, and in particular the music of the Swing era. Many of the ballrooms he recalls are no longer with us but their memory remains fresh in the mind.

The next Waltz will be a Quickstep

Dancing – in large or small ballrooms – was without a doubt a marvellous source of enjoyment from the Twenties to the Fifties. And performing all the different kinds of dance steps was the goal of Northern Ireland's huge following of the authentic strict tempo style.

Although the disco era now allows each person to form his or her own independent dancing style, the aim used to be partnership. The gentleman's responsibility was to initiate and control the progress of the dance while moving forward. The lady then moved backwards in total response to the male partner's guidance and choice of steps.

Ladies seemed to accept the formality and tradition of dancing etiquette. This apparent male domination did not seem to cause the resentment which might be justified with today's emphasis on women's rights.

Ballroom dancing was very popular and each partner took pride in achieving the best possible standard. Those who took pure dancing seriously might consider progression to a bronze medal or beyond. People of all ages danced and there was a marvellous social mix.

Belfast contained all manner of dance establishments. Great numbers flocked to the Plaza, Albert White's, the Orpheus and the Floral Hall. The Plaza proudly provided two bands for the evening's patrons, and late-night buses left the tired dancers home at the end of busy weekend dances. After a Saturday night dance at Bellevue's Floral Hall, buses completed a circular tour which left you within easy walking distance from your home wherever you lived in the city.

At the Orpheus in York Street, piano magic was supplied by Billy White, and the ladies appreciated the sentimental crooning of Archie Coates. In fact his singing style was so appealing that the lady dancers had eyes for Archie only when he made his appearance at the microphone on the bandstand. An advertisement in July 1944 for the Rinkha Ballroom in Islandmagee read:

Louisa Moe dancing with the Hawaiian Serenaders in 1944.

Just after the war Archie went to England as vocalist with Felix Mendelssohn and his Hawaiian Serenaders. He returned to his native Ulster's music scene and became associated with Sammy Mitchell and the Melotones. I was delighted to hear that Archie is still here and living in

Belfast where he still sings. In fact he appeared on *Day by Day* to talk about the old days early in 1982. And there was an extraordinary coincidence that morning. When the programme trail was broadcast earlier that morning, Felix Mendelssohn's former manager Ian Maxfield heard

Archie's name and immediately phoned the BBC. Ian was staying overnight on his first visit to the Province for many years and he readily accepted an invitation to meet Archie again in the studio. When Ian walked in during the programme it caught Archie completely by surprise, and their re-union took place on the air, the first time they had met for over thirty years.

Name bands also visited the province to give greater variety. I remember Joe Loss at the Floral Hall, and Nat Gonella and his New Georgians in the Ulster Hall. One summer's evening Oscar Rabin played at Caproni's at Bangor. Although the band was noted for its recordings in strict tempo style, the dancers stopped and gathered round the bandstand to hear the musicians play swing tunes in marvellous style.

Other towns had their dance halls too. During a week's stay in Londonderry I enjoyed dances in the Corinthian and in the Guildhall. Depending on age each of us will have memories of special favourite locations. Holiday-makers enjoyed the Arcadia in Portrush with its windows overlooking the sea. On a bright summer's evening you could easily imagine that you were dancing on board a luxury ocean liner. It seemed as though Dave Glover was always there to provide the Arcadia's music.

Of course you had to learn to dance and many were taught at places run by famous names like Betty Staff, Sammy Leckey or Sammy Osborne. There were fondly remembered places such as Foster's Windsor School of Dancing. The famous John Dossor was my own teacher and even today when I hear records of Victor Sylvester and his Ballroom Orchestra, the atmosphere of those dance lessons comes back to me very clearly. As I recall it, the classes were nearly always based on the music of Victor Sylvester. Our weekly classes progressed beyond the standard Waltz, Quickstep and Slow Foxtrot to the exotic Latin American rhythms of the Tango, Rhumba and Samba. Our vocabulary was extended to enable us to discuss with confidence the Quarter Turn, the Lock and the Chassé.

Archie Coates (centre) and Ian Maxfield (right) meet again after thirty years.

* * *

'May I have this dance please?'

Translated into the less formal American style:

'Are ye dancin'?'

'Are ye askin'?'

'Yeah, I'm askin'.'

'Then I'm dancin'.'

* * *

'We're having some Victor Silvester weather this winter: snow, snow, thick thick snow.'

(Slow, slow, quick quick, slow.)

* * *

Advice from an 'expert' on the best places to go dancing:

'No-one ever goes to that dance hall now – it's too crowded!'

* * *

Two dancers discussing the pianist in the band:

'What do you think of his execution?' asked the first.

'I'm all in favour of it,' was the cool response of the second.

* * *

Description of a flashy tie worn by one man at a dance:

'You wouldn't be caught wearing that tie at twelve o'clock at night at the bottom of a coalmine during a total eclipse of the moon.'

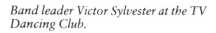

Band leader Victor Sylvester at the TV Dancing Club.

18

Many dance programmes also featured set dances carried forward from a previous generation – the Military Twostep, Pride of Erin, St Bernard's Waltz and the Moonlight Saunter. The newer generation were captivated by the American influence of Jive with practical demonstrations by off-duty visiting GIs.

The ladies always looked their best at dances. Attractive dresses, careful make-up and well-groomed hair styles all added greater glamour to the occasion. Men dressed in suits and ties with shoes always black and freshly polished.

I recall an embarrassing moment at a crowded dance. Men's trousers had turn-ups and one of mine provided the unwary trap for a lady's high heel. While trying to move quickly past her I brought both the lady and her partner crashing to the floor. I would like to have apologised but we all became separated in the crowd. I was relieved to find no sign of injury when the dancers left the floor.

All sorts of devices were used to help people mix. The occasional Ladies' Choice was called to prevent them becoming 'wallflowers' which could easily happen if very

few men were present. The announcement of a Paul Jones or General Excuse Me heralded a change of partner each time the music stopped. It was my experience that many of the plumper ladies were the best dancers and seemed very light on their feet. I can claim – as so many others can – that I met my lifelong partner at a dance. And as an afterthought, I'd better say, she isn't in the heavyweight class!

You need a lot of energy to keep up the pace of ballroom dancing. The steps involved allowed movement across the floor with everyone going in the same basic direction. In an evening you covered quite a distance and by the time of the last waltz you appreciated the chance to slow down. The band would finish by playing a song with an appropriate title like 'Who's Taking You Home Tonight?'

While one tends to remember the larger commercial ballrooms attended by huge crowds, let us not forget the occasional small dance held in the local scout or band hall. I look back with a smile when I recall an amateur Master of Ceremonies announcing the next item for the dancers. He created confusion as well as laughter when he announced: 'Ladies and gentlemen. The next Waltz will be a Quickstep.'

Now the book said to put my LF forward in PP moving LOD diagonal to wall. RF forward. But ... er ... which is my LF?

Dance cards were essential to help you remember which partner you had promised which dance.

THE INCORPORATED ACCOUNTANTS' BELFAST AND DISTRICT SOCIETY

Students' Section.

DANCE

CARLTON
RESTAURANT
BELFAST

January, 1937

mirth

Dances.

1. Valse.
2. One-Step.
3. Fox Trot.
4. Valse.
5. Fox Trot.
6. One-Step
7. Valse.
8. Fox Trot.
9. Supper Dance.
10. One-Step
11. Fox Trot.
12. One-Step.
13. Valse—Leap Year.
14. Fox Trot.
15. Lancers.
16. Valse.
17. One-Step.
18. Valse.

Engagements.

1.
2.
3.
4.
5.
6.
7.
8.
9.
10.
11.
12.
13.
14.
15.
16.
17.
18.

Dance Programme.

1. Quick Step
2. Waltz
3. Fox Trot
4. Jumble Dance
5. Palais Glide
6. Hesitation Waltz
7. Fox Trot
8. Novelty Dance (Quick Step)
9. Valeta
10. Lancers
11. Quick Step
12. Waltz
13. Fox Trot
14. Novelty Dance (Fox Trot)
15. Jumble Dance
16. Waltz
17. Military Two Step
18. Valeta
19. Palais Glide
22. Fox Trot
23. Hesitation Waltz
24. Fox Trot
Waltz
Extras as requested

M.C.'s.—Mr. J. D. Tem.
Mr. Norman
Mr. W. C.

Slow Fox-Trot—Feather Step.

Fred Bell

Like Roy Irvine and Charlie Gallagher, Fred Bell has been a dedicated follower of fashion in the dance band sense for many decades now. If his early ambitions to become a full-time musician were not to be realised, his talents as a serious and critical listener have developed steadily over the years. Now retired, after a lifetime in a variety of jobs, Fred likes to share his memories of the great British dance bands. He loves them all, but one man and his music in particular.

In the Mood

One of my earliest ambitions was to learn to play the piano. But times were hard back in the 1920s and we couldn't afford a piano, so I had to think of something else. I kept my eyes open and was lucky enough to pick up a drum-kit instead. It was a second-hand set and it only cost a couple of quid but at the age of seventeen it was good enough. From then on drumming was the thing.

I even got three friends to join me and set up a small band. We used to play all over the place in the late Twenties and in the Thirties: dances, concerts, church halls and sports clubs. In fact if I'd had my own way I'd have had a go at making music my full-time job, but that idea didn't go down well at home. So instead of music all the way I served my time in a wholesale warehouse in Rosemary Street, and hated every minute of it. I got out when I could and found a job as a cost clerk in the Shipyard. That was during the day, but at night at least I could concentrate on my first love – music.

Sometimes there was the chance to play with other bands, like Albert Gray's. I can remember a couple of dinner dances in Thompson's. It was all Quick-steps, Slow Foxtrots, Waltzes and Tangos then. We played all the standards of the day, usually in sets of three. But when I wasn't playing dance music at night I was usually at home tuned in to the old BBC Light Programme. Every night, Monday to Friday, from 10.30 p.m. till midnight, all the top British bands could be heard coming live from the big hotels and ballrooms in London. The bands

usually did a full week so if you couldn't listen in every night you usually managed to hear a bit of it on other nights.

It must have been the radio, and what was available on records, that developed my life-long passion for dance music. The bands which broadcast evey night were household names, and so were the places they broadcast from, like Jack Hylton from the Savoy, or Sydney Lipton

June, 1935

AMBROSE'S TIGER RAG !
SENSATIONAL RECORD OF THE YEAR

and his Orchestra from Grosvenor House in Mayfair. And the Mayfair Hotel featured the music of Ambrose, often with vocalist Anne Shelton. It's hard to recall all the names but I couldn't leave out such famous musical personalities as Roy Fox, Harry Roy, Oscar Rabin, Maurice Winnick and Lew Stone. Al Bowlly was a regular featured singer with Lew Stone. Tragically he was killed not long afterwards in the blitz when a landmine blew up close to his flat in Central London.

24

But there is one name I haven't mentioned. For me the best of them all, Joe Loss. I can't say how many times I heard the great Joe Loss Band broadcasting from the Astoria Ballroom on the Charing Cross Road. But since then he always has been, and still is, my number one. Whenever I listen to a top-line band I try to listen with as keen an ear as possible. I listen beyond the top line to what's going on underneath. For me there has always been something more in the music of Joe Loss.

The band has been over here in Northern Ireland on a number of occasions, but I actually met Joe for the first time in Glasgow just after Christmas in 1941. He was resident for a week at Green's Playhouse Ballroom in Renfrew Street, and I sat for the first three nights in the right-hand front corner of the balcony, just about as near as I could get to the stage. I must have been almost hanging over the edge because at the end of the National Anthem on the third night, Joe turned and pointed his baton at me and called up: 'Would you wait there a moment.' At first I didn't realise that he was talking to me. But he suddenly appeared beside me. He told me he'd noticed that I hadn't danced at all and that I seemed to be paying a lot of attention to the music. I couldn't believe it was happening when he invited me backstage. And that was the start of a life-long friendship.

In fact I must have had some nerve because later that week Joe's personnel manager Charlie Boehm was present when I suggested a change in the band's opening routine. They normally opened with a tune called 'Make Believe Ballroom' and then went into 'In the Mood' followed by 'Woodchoppers Ball'. Having watched the reaction of the crowd that week in Glasgow I felt that they would have a better impact with 'In the Mood' first, and I told Joe and Charlie so. The next night they kicked off with 'In the Mood' and that has been the band's signature tune ever since.

When the war ended, the London Hotel bands started touring, first around England and then to Dublin and Belfast. Many of them appeared in the Grand Opera

FLORAL HALL
HAZELWOOD

SEASON 1940

Dancing and Cabaret
EVERY EVENING
ALEX MONAGHAN AND HIS BAND

House. They usually appeared for a full week with two performances nightly. Variety acts filled the first half of these shows and the bands took over for the second half. I can remember Billy Cotton being here, and Charlie Kunz, the pianist, also had a band here. Joe Loss came to the Opera House twice, once with the marvellous Monte Rey as featured vocalist. Whenever Joe Loss and the band appeared I never missed a chance to be there, not only in the Opera House but in the Floral Hall and in Caproni's. His last visit to Belfast was in the late Fifties and was an appearance in the Ulster Hall. Unfortunately there wasn't the customary capacity crowd because there was a lightning transport strike that day and many fans were unable to get into town that night.

The Ritz Cinema, which was opened in November 1936, also had many live shows. The one I remember best, just after it opened, was when Ken 'Snakehips' Johnson came over. Ken was a West Indian who had come to Britain in 1929 and had turned to band-leading with great success. He was an immaculate character who wore not only white tie and tails, but white shoes to complete the effect. He was as thin as a rake and got the nickname 'Snakehips' because of his agility as a dancer. He didn't play in the band himself. It was led by trumpeter Leslie Thompson and was a brilliant group. The female singer was another West Indian, Nina Mae McKinney, and the Ritz was packed to capacity. As well as being a big audience it was an enthusiastic one and the atmosphere was electric. Sadly, like Al Bowlly, 'Snakehips' too became a war casualty when a bomb hit the Café de Paris in March 1941. Both he and the tenor saxophone player Dave Williams were killed. While many of the great band leaders of the Thirties are no longer with us, it's good to know that there still remains a legacy of the past in the many fine records they made.

Charlie Gallagher

There are some remarkable similarities in the careers and interests of Roy Irvine and Charlie Gallagher. While Charlie was born in Derry, he spent most of his working life in the Post Office, moving from engineering to personnel management. But the greatest thing they have in common is their love of jazz and the big bands. Charlie is an acknowledged authority on the music of Glenn Miller and, in particular, the American Band of the Allied Expeditionary Force. But he has many other interests as well. A qualified glider pilot, he is also the co-founder and architect of an aviation society devoted to the US Army 8th Air Force in World War II. His achievements have been recognised by his special award from the US Airforce for his outstanding contribution to Anglo-American relations. Last year saw the publication of his combined autobiography and social history of Derry from 1920 to 1945: 'Acorns and Oakleaves'.

26

Stars, Stripes & Shamrocks

Who would have realised that an event which happened far away in the Pacific on 7 December 1941 would have a considerable impact on the people of Northern Ireland. On that day the Japanese attacked the American Pacific Fleet at Pearl Harbour in the Phillipines. And that was how the United States entered the Second World War.

On 26 January 1942, a bemused Private First Class of the US Army stepped gingerly onto the Pollock Dock, in Belfast's dockland. Private M. H. Henke was the first of a trickle which became a river, and then a flood, of khaki-clad troops wearing strangely-shaped headgear, rubber-soled boots, fatigue coveralls, zip-fastened combat jackets, and hung about with knives, whistles, holsters and automatic weapons, or drove an assortment of trucks ranging from multi-wheel articulated giants, to a little four-seater resembling a cross between a Model T Ford and a soap-box, which they called a Jeep.

I remember the first parade of the American troops through Derry. They seemed to have great difficulty in keeping in step, and then the reason why became apparent. Their rubber-soled footwear made practically no sound on the road surface, so that their ears had no reference to their steps. It had an eerie, almost comic, effect, this column of marching men striding soundlessly through the streets. Their discipline, too, seemed lax to our eyes. I heard a soldier call out to an officer in one of their camps, 'Hey, Lieutenant, what time you got?' The Lieutenant replied, 'Four thirty,' whereupon the trooper shook his head and said, 'Goddamit! I'll be late for chow.'

By the summer of 1943, there was hardly a town or village in Northern Ireland which did not have its quota of GIs, as the troops were called. Inevitably the presence of nearly 200,000 American servicemen wrought a tremendous change in the social life and habits of the people of the Province. We became accustomed to the Southern drawl, the flat, hard vowels of the New Englander and the Runyonesque turn of phrase of the New Yorker.

Hershey chocolate bars, O'Henry bars, Wrigley's chewing gum, Prince Albert tobacco, Chesterfield, Camel and Lucky Strike cigarettes, and of course, bananas, oranges and nylons became 'currency'. The Americans were unbelievably generous, especially towards children. On the great American holidays of Thanksgiving, Independence Day and Labor Day, they invited thousands of children to parties on their bases and stations. Orphanages, too, benefited from their bounty, especially at Christmas.

Not everything in Northern Ireland was to their liking, however, particularly the weather – 'Nine months winter and three months bad weather makes up the year.'

'Six months of the year Lough Foyle is in County Derry, the other six months County Derry is in Lough Foyle.'

However, their welcome into the Irish homes where

'Every American soldier an ambassador of good will' was the Army's advice to the 'doughboys'. These two trainees are doing their bit in Northern Ireland.

many thousands of them were treated like members of the family, kindled friendships which are maintained even today, forty years on.

One way of taking their minds off the drawbacks of life in the Province was the entertainment they brought with them, in particular their music. Possibly the first American art form to be exported to Europe was Jazz.

Jazz first arrived in the UK and on the continent in the 1920s, and names like Duke Ellington and Louis Armstrong were well known, but when the GIs hit the scene, fresh from the dance halls and ballrooms of Chicago, Kansas City, San Francisco, New Orleans, Milwaukee or New York's Harlem, they brought with them the Lindy Hop, the Big Apple, the Suzy Q, all of which came under the collective name of Jitterbugging. In Derry, the Clarendon Hall featured a band which was nearest to the American style, and there we stood, eyes out on stalks, as we watched the GIs and sailors whose generic nickname was 'Gobs', lead Derry girls through the frenetic steps of numbers like 'In the Mood', 'Apple Honey' or 'Woodchoppers Ball', feet and skirts aflying.

Most bases and camps had their own dance bands, and the big American record companies made special recordings called 'V. discs' which they supplied free to American units, and the music of Benny Goodman, Artie Shaw, Tommy Dorsey, Harry James and many others was piped throughout the Army, Navy and Airforce Stations all day long.

Naturally, the thoughts of hundreds of thousands of young, fit and virile young men turned to girls. Even in the remotest villages of the Sperrins, the Mournes, or in the fastnesses of Fermanagh, girls of all shapes, sizes and ages, found themselves being squired around by eager GIs. Many of these young ladies had never been on a date before, and had to learn the tricks of unarmed combat fast! Others who had resigned themselves to a place 'on the shelf' grabbed their chances – and their men – with both arms.

Not all of the girls, however, took kindly to the Yanks.

As Mama Hands up a Bowl of Water, Her Children Inspect an American Tank—What Would They Give to Drive It!

More than likely the crew has been invited into the thatched farmhouse for tea or dinner. But tea is rationed, and a good dinner costs the housewife most of her week's meat allotment. The Army, therefore, discourages acceptance of Ulster hospitality.

('National Geographic', August 1943)

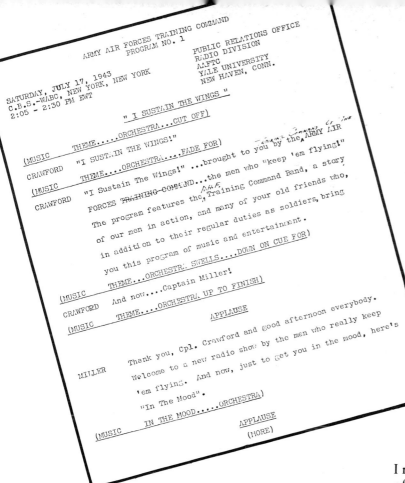

ARMY AIR FORCES TRAINING COMMAND
PROGRAM NO. 1

PUBLIC RELATIONS OFFICE
RADIO DIVISION
AAFTC
YALE UNIVERSITY
NEW HAVEN, CONN.

SATURDAY, JULY 17, 1943
C.B.S.-WABC, NEW YORK, NEW YORK
2:05 - 2:30 PM EWT

" I SUSTAIN THE WINGS "

(MUSIC   THEME.....ORCHESTRA...CUT OFF)

CRAWFORD   "I SUSTAIN THE WINGS!"

(MUSIC   THEME....ORCHESTRA....FADE FOR)

CRAWFORD   "I Sustain The Wings!" ...brought to you by the ARMY AIR
            FORCES TRAINING COMMAND...the men who "keep 'em flying!"
            The program features the AAF Training Command Band, a story
            of our men in action, and many of your old friends who,
            in addition to their regular duties as soldiers, bring
            you this program of music and entertainment.

(MUSIC   THEME...ORCHESTRA SWELLS....DOWN ON CUE FOR)

CRAWFORD   And now....Captain Miller!

(MUSIC   THEME....ORCHESTRA UP TO FINISH)

                          APPLAUSE

MILLER   Thank you, Cpl. Crawford and good afternoon everybody.
            Welcome to a new radio show by the men who really keep
            'em flying. And now, just to get you in the mood, here's
            "In The Mood".

(MUSIC   IN THE MOOD.....ORCHESTRA)

                          APPLAUSE
                          (MORE)

*Above: Copy of the actual script of 'I Sustain
the Wings' broadcast 17 July 1943.*

*Right: Glen Miller in uniform.
(USAF photo)*

*Opposite: Glenn Miller (on trombone) leads
the band. (USAF photo)*

I recall travelling in a bus from the Waterside to the City
of Derry one night during the blackout. The conductor
was standing on the rear step, peering out into the
darkness, and calling out the stops. 'Dungiven Road',
'Spencer Road', 'Carlisle Square', intoned the conductor,
and as each girl got out, a group of American sailors
called, 'Fifth Avenue, this is where you get off, lady',
'Forty-second Street, this is where you get off, lady,'
'Times Square, this is where you get off, lady', until one of
the last girls to alight turned and snapped: 'Pearl
Harbour! That's where youse got off.'

As the build up for D-Day – the code name for Invasion
Day – reached its peak, we suddenly noticed the

31

countryside becoming quieter. In the stillness of the May nights, we heard the growl of truck engines labouring in low gear, the heavily-loaded vehicles set off on their journeys to the docks and ferries – the first stage of their trip to Hitler's Fortress Europa.

In the mornings, the camps were curiously silent and still. Inside the Nissen huts notices and orders still hung on the walls. The pictures and reproductions of the Esquire pin-ups remained after the beds and bunks had gone. In the pubs and cafés, we missed the goodnatured banter of Al and Joe, the wisecracks of South Side Benny and the stolid good sense of 'Swede' Larsen.

In the months following the invasion, information slowly trickled back. The 82nd Airborne, which had trained near Castledawson, was dropped into a cauldron of fire at St Mère Église and suffered many casualties. The Second, Fifth and Eighth Infantry Divisions sustained heavy losses during the D-Day landings, and subsequently at the Battle of St Lô.

Even today, the sound of the late, great Glenn Miller's Army Air Force Band on a record can instantly evoke the flavour and atmosphere of those times.

Miller had been the most popular band leader in America, and after volunteering for the Services, was commissioned a Captain in the Army. He was assigned to the Air Services Training Command, and after assembling an orchestra of the finest musicians available, he broadcast coast to coast in the United States for a year in a programme called *I Sustain The Wings* aimed at recruiting for the Air Force. By May 1944, there were over a million and a half GIs in the UK, and the American Band of the Allied Expeditionary Force, as it became known, was sent to England as a morale booster for the troops.

For the next five months in draughty hangars, on remote bases, in clubs and halls, the music of the superb AEF Band transported lonely, homesick men back to the USA. The proverbial pin could have been heard to drop when Sergeant Johnny Desmond's warm, vibrant voice

This page and opposite: some of the graffiti left behind by the American servicemen.

sang of love – unrequited or fulfilled – against the lush background of arrangements by Sergeants Jerry Gray, Mel Powell and Norman Leyden. When the Uptown Hall Gang led by pianist Mel Powell took over, the audience fairly rocked as they belted out 'My Guy's Come Back!' or 'Blue Skies', and the Swing Shift arrangements of 'Mission to Moscow' and 'In the Mood' had them screaming for more. The band also broadcast three times weekly on the BBC, and Johnny Desmond did a regular broadcast called *A Soldier and a Song*. Millions of listeners eagerly followed these programmes which were usually transmitted from the band's base at Bedford.

On 13 August 1944, the entire orchestra, singers and announcers flew into Langford Lodge in two C.47 Dakotas. They were driven into Belfast in buses, and played to a capacity crowd in the Plaza, which was then the American Red Cross Club. They then went back to Langford Lodge, and played to an audience of fifteen hundred GIs and their friends in the camp theatre before flying back to England.

A few months later, on 15 December, Major Miller was offered a lift to Paris in a small single-engined aircraft – a UC64 Norseman. It was a very foggy day, and all regular Transport Command planes were grounded. Miller accepted the lift, but neither he nor the other two occupants of the machine were even seen again, nor was any wreckage ever found.

The war dragged on for another year and a half, but the end was inevitable, although many hundreds of thousands were still to die. Finally Germany surrendered, and an uneasy peace descended upon Europe. The GIs and their war-brides went back to the USA, but they left a legacy of memories, and traces of their stay amongst us are still to be seen on derelict airfields, in rusting and rotting Nissen huts in remote fields and copses, and in faded graffiti on crumbling walls – *'Neither Cycles, nor Americans to be leant against this wall'*, *'Los Angeles City Limits'*, *'Mess Site! Eat all you can When, and If, you get it!'*

Louis Gilbert

Louis Gilbert is in many ways our local memory man. He was born in the Stranmillis area of Belfast and doesn't mind admitting that that event occurred some seventy years ago. For Louis the best part of a long working life was when he ran the 'Belfast Telegraph' library for ten years until 1978. His love of entertainment in its widest sense is one of the hallmarks of his weekly chats on 'Day by Day'. Both as a performer himself and as a social historian he knows well how to entertain. Perhaps theatre is his greatest love, and for Louis that means the silver screen as well — both silent, as it started out, and later with the addition of sound.

Come to the Show

Talking pictures first came to Belfast in the late summer of 1929. The Picture House on Royal Avenue – which had been showing silent films for more than ten years – installed an expensive sound system. In future, all films were to have dialogue and music, instead of captions telling audiences what the characters were saying.

For eight weeks, long queues formed in Royal Avenue four times each weekday. Belfast folk waited patiently to get into the cinema, to see and hear Al Jolson talking and making music in *The Singing Fool*; the first full-length talkie to be shown here.

The auditorium of the Picture House had been decorated for the occasion. People sat in semi-darkness, waiting to witness the wonder that had come to Northern Ireland. They listened to harsh recorded music coming from behind the screen. The pit, where David Curry and the Picture House Orchestra had performed every day for years, was filled with artificial palm trees.

At that time the silent cinema was big business in Ulster. The talkies were the first major change in an entertainment industry that had been successful for a decade. Many questions were asked. Why change something that is financially strong? Would the talkies survive long enough to risk the investment in sound equipment? What would happen to the hundreds of musicians who were earning their living in Ulster's picture houses?

Proprietors and cinema managers watched the Royal Avenue experiment with great interest and it soon became evident to them that the talking pictures from America were in Ulster to stay. The long queues at the Picture House, the happy reaction of cinemagoers to loud American speech, tinny American music, and emotional American stories, assured them that talking pictures were the natural development of silent films. The silent cinema industry, so popular and prosperous since the end of the First World War, had come to an end.

The only home amusement in the 1920s was the gramophone with the horn-shaped speaker and records with a single song, or piece of music, on each side. The picture houses, theatres, concert halls and ballrooms, were the main places of entertainment, and the silent cinema was, by far, the most popular.

Every evening, Belfast's down-town cinemas were filled to capacity and had long queues of people waiting outside. Performances were continuous from two in the afternoon until half past ten. Seat prices ranged from sixpence to 1s 6d in the afternoon and from a shilling to a half crown in the evening.

In well-populated districts, outside the city centre, there were a number of small picture houses known as family cinemas. They attracted the same local people each week and performed twice nightly with a penny matinee for children on Saturday afternoons.

Belfast's most luxurious picture house then was the Classic Cinema in Castle Lane. Built in 1924, it was large,

The Classic Cinema

—

The Centre
of
Cinema Art

"Swing that Organ"

WHAT a remark, what a declaration! — if it is a declaration. Am I to go in for " strong man " stuff? That is the latest demand made upon me — " Swing that Organ." What does it mean? " To swing or not to swing?" that is the question; and I, as usual, must try and answer it. Just like you, I have been watching with great curiosity — and, in my case, complete ignorance — the mystifying controversy on " swing music." First of all I thought it was—er—variations of the tune " The Daring Young Man on the Flying Trapeze," but no, it really couldn't be that, because in the " Organ Grinder's Swing " it surely meant the rhythm the monkey-man put into turnin' the old 'andle. Then again, there was the " Swing Patrol," which may or may not be connected with the guard taking care of the swing boats at the fair. But NO! (cue for song " At Dawning ") on listening to numbers of radio programmes, I gather that " Swing " is j st the latest mood taken by that very temperamental old man, JAZZ. To my great amusement and pleasure I received several letters from radio " swing " fans offering congratulations on my " swing " numbers. (To what depths of degradation have I sunk? Woe is me! I swing — to and fro with the greatest of ease). Many of our gayer friends in the Classic Club — sorry! — Cinema, are pressing me to do a whole presentation on SWING. " Go on, Leslie, do?" " No, I won't !" " Oh, please do, we'd love it." " Well, perhaps sometime."

I was delighted to have to cough up five bob so promptly. Last month's programmes hadn't been in circulation more than a week when your welcome replies started to roll in. And they were all good stuff, both sensible and workable. The only criticism I can make is that very few titles were what I call intriguing. I mean the kind of title which conceals something and causes one to think before it fades and is forgotten. To obtain a really good title is very, very difficult. You read what the folks who have the job of titling films have to say about it ! Mr Louis Gilbert of Stranmillis who, by the way, sent a whole string of titles, is the laddie who had the pleasure of seeing his own title on the screen. It so happened that I was just about to present a show I called ": The 'Hits ' of Yesterday," and I promptly tacked on his suggestion " Forgotten Favou= rites " as being a possibly better title — and there you are....Good for Louis !

SEE YOU AT THE CLASSIC

ROYAL CINEMA (ARTHUR SQUARE) BELFAST

Our films

The
World's Championship Fight
DEMPSEY v. TUNNEY

This film exclusive to the Royal

WEEK COMMENCING
OCTOBER 18th

Monthly Magazine

OCTOBER, 1926

well-ventilated, and comfortable. The films shown were the latest from Hollywood and screened for the first time in Belfast. Pauline Frederick, Lilian Gish, Mary Pickford, Clara Bow, Douglas Fairbanks, Ronald Coleman, John Gilbert, Ramon Navarro and the great Greta Garbo were stars who thrilled audiences at the Classic in film stories which lifted people high above their drab surroundings and the ordinary existence that many of them knew.

To create the right atmosphere for the Hollywood dream machine, the Classic Cinema Orchestra, thirty talented musicians under the direction of T.S. Clark-Brown, performed music in keeping with the action on the screen. And when the orchestra had a break, Cecil Chadwick accompanied the film on the mighty Wurlitzer organ.

Each show consisted of two films and a musical interlude aptly called 'Thirty Melodious Minutes', in which the orchestra and organ played classical, light, and jazz music, all greatly appreciated by the audience.

The Royal Cinema at Arthur Square was another popular picture house. Owned by Warden Ltd, the proprietors of the Grand Opera House, it had once been the Theatre Royal, and managed to retain some of the atmosphere and appearance of the old theatre. It was less comfortable than the Classic but it screened many great films. *The Covered Wagon* and Charlie Chaplin's *Goldrush* got their first Belfast showing there. F.H. Doherty and his orchestra accompanied all the films with suitable music but they did not provide an interlude. The music was heard but the musicians were unseen in the pit below the stage; a stage where, years before, great actors and actresses had often performed.

Young people patronised the Imperial Picture House in Cornmarket because it screened love stories and romantic westerns. Its orchestra, under Victor Norman, was more of a jazz band, and it provided a musical interlude with the popular music the younger generation wanted to hear.

The Imperial did have one drawback however – it was

long, narrow and uncomfortable. The orchestra pit was at ground level, and with twenty musicians in it, the screen was high on the wall, so that people in the first few rows of the stalls had to look upwards continually, and often left the cinema with a stiff neck. There was a small roped-off area at the back of the stalls where patrons waited for a seat – a purgatory between a street queue and a plush red stalls seat. It was known as the cow pen.

These three cinemas, and the Picture House on Royal Avenue, had select cafés serving all meals from morning coffee to supper. People living in the suburbs and nearby country towns came direct from work to the pictures. A high tea in the café cost 1s 6d and a seat in the stalls a shilling – a good night out for a half crown.

The Lyric Cinema in High Street was less popular and had formerly been the Panoptican. It was possible to get a seat there when the other down-town cinemas were full and it saw real-life drama when an employee once hanged himself there. But even a change of name failed to chase people's fears.

Some smaller cinemas, in the city centre, had historical associations. The Central Picture House in Smithfield stood on the site of Heffron's National Theatre. The Alhambra in North Street was once Willie John Ashcroft's music hall. The Coliseum, on the Grosvenor Road, knew barnstorming melodrama when it was the Alexandra Theatre. The Kelvin Cinema, in College Square East, was erected on the site of a house where Lord Kelvin was born, and the Gaiety Theatre in Upper North Street had been the home of minstrel shows and local concert parties.

In most areas of Belfast you hardly needed to go into the city for your entertainment. If you lived in Ballymacarrett, for instance, you had a choice of three cinemas on the Newtownards Road alone – the Old Princess, the Popular Picture House and the New Princess Picture Palace. And there was the Mountpottinger Picturedrome, which catered for those who were young and in love, with romantic stories and soft sweet music played by Mitchell

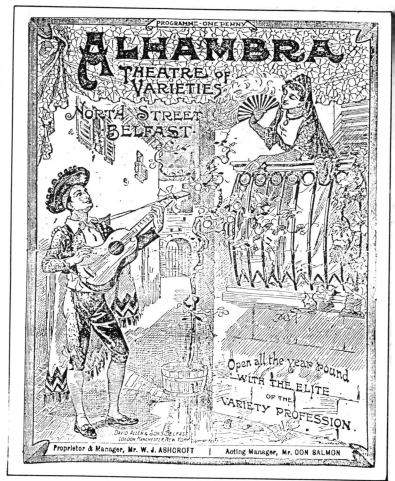

The Alhambra Theatre of Varieties met the same fate as many other music halls in Britain and Ireland: after operating for many years as a cinema it was demolished to make way for shops.

Crowley and a small orchestra. So popular in fact was cinema entertainment in East Belfast that a Unionist Club on the Woodstock Road turned its main hall into the successful Willowfield Picture House.

Mr Joe McKibben – a Shankill Road grocer – had taken advantage of the silent cinema boom by building two picture houses in his own district – the West End Cinema and the Shankill Picturedrome. He crossed the religious divide and opened the Diamond Picture House on the Falls Road and followed with the Midland Picture House in Canning Street. Patrons who were short of cash could gain admission to any of these cinemas by presenting jam pots at the pay box. Mr McKibben with some enterprise turned these into cash through his grocery business.

The Antrim Road had a very select cinema – the Lyceum – at the corner of New Lodge Road. It was a popular house and the first, outside the city centre, to install sound equipment. The Crumlin Picture House screened cowboy films almost exclusively, which is why it was known locally as 'The Ranch'. The Duncairn Picture House on Duncairn Gardens and the Queens on York Road were patronised exclusively by local people.

The Arcadian Cinema in Albert Street was affectionately known as 'The Cage', why I don't know. The Sandro Cinema on Sandy Row and the Clonard Picture House on the Falls Road complete a list of small cinemas that brought a lot of happy entertainment to Belfast folk in the days of silent pictures.

In the 1930s, the change was rapid. All the cinemas in down-town Belfast installed sound systems. Fewer silent pictures were made in Hollywood and Elstree, as popular actors and actresses spoke for the first time on the screen. Sometimes Belfast people were amused, sometimes shocked, but by 1935 there was not a silent cinema in Ulster, not a musician employed in any picture house.

New luxurious cinemas were built in the suburbs and on any available city-centre site. Union Cinemas – a British company – erected the Ritz, a massive cine-variety theatre across the road from Church House. Gracie Fields performed the opening ceremony. It had a Compton organ that rose illuminated from the orchestra pit. Joseph Seal not only pleased Belfast audiences for years, but he broadcast from the Ritz every week in the old BBC Home Service.

Union Cinemas also built the Majestic on the Lisburn Road and the Strand at Strandtown. Mr Michael Curran of the Lyceum erected luxury cinemas for each of his sons – the Regal at Balmoral, the Broadway on the Falls Road, the Astoria on the Upper Newtownards Road and the Capitol on the Antrim Road. He then bought the huge Tonic Cinema in Bangor and the Apollo on the Ormeau Road.

By 1938 there were sound cinemas on all the main roads in Belfast. On the Shankill, Joe McKibben – who had long since stopped using jam pots for admission – had competition from the large Stadium Cinema, but his two smaller picture houses survived. What flamboyant names these new cinemas had: Metro, Castle, Ambassador, Curzon, Windsor, Forum, Savoy and Troxy.

But Belfast's theatres did not have the success or popularity the cinemas experienced. Back in the 1920s, they were able to compete with silent picture houses. The Grand Opera House presented a different touring company each week. Sometimes it was a successful play with a London cast, on other occasions plays were tried out in Belfast prior to London presentation.

Some companies paid annual visits to the Opera House. The Birmingham Repertory Theatre presented a week of George Bernard Shaw with a different play each evening. The Abbey Theatre Company staged a season of Irish plays and the Ulster Literary Theatre presented the latest in Ulster drama and comedy. Fred Warden's pantomimes ran for six weeks each Christmas.

The Carl Rosa and D'Oyly Carte Opera Companies, Chappel & Co's presentation of *Lilac Time* and big musical comedies from London with huge casts always filled the Opera House to capacity during their stay.

Programme

17 May 1937

Prices ranged from 5s 9d for the front stalls and the dress circle down to one shilling for the gallery. Performances started at 7.30 pm, though patrons could, if they wished, take advantage of the 'early door' in Glengall Street. It cost an extra threepence, but as well as getting you in first, it also gave you the chance of seeing the actors and actresses arriving at the stage door. On Friday evenings, people in the stalls and circle wore evening dress and travelled by tram. On Saturdays students and young people packed 'the gods' and made their own entertainment until the programme began.

The Royal Hippodrome presented top variety and revue, twice nightly, each week. George Dobler, the very popular manager, would stand at the main entrance before each performance wearing evening dress and raising his top hat as he graciously welcomed patrons to the stalls and circle. Layton & Johnston, Harry Lauder, Billy Bennett, the Houston Sisters, Will Fyffe, Florrie Forde, Randolph Sutton, Jimmy O'Dea and Gertie Gitana are some of the performers who enjoyed great popularity at the Hippodrome.

Variety theatres suffered acutely when sound cinemas took some of their supporters. Others stayed at home because of a different kind of competition; the new wireless programmes.

Early in 1930, the Royal Hippodrome installed sound equipment and became another cinema. The Grand Opera House changed to a variety hall as well as a serious theatre, and many of the Hippodrome stars made their appearances there during occasional variety seasons in the 1930s.

The Empire Theatre in Victoria Square also had difficulty competing with the talking pictures but somehow it survived the lean 1930s. It attracted those Hippodrome patrons who preferred music hall to cinema. Many of the second-rate touring revues presented there were described as 'daring and exotic'. Titles like *Scandals of Buenos Aires, Ladies of the Night,* and *A Night in Paris* attracted curious audiences.

Composer and songwriter Irving Berlin (seated, on the left, in civilian clothes) on a visit to the Opera House during the war years.

The Empire Theatre continued to present variety and drama until the 1960s, when it was knocked down to make room for a department store.

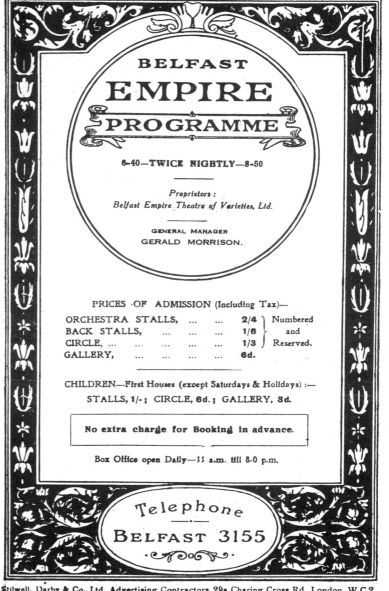

EMPIRE THEATRE, BELFAST

Week commencing MONDAY the 21st of JANUARY, 1935
TWICE NIGHTLY at 6.40 and 8.50

RICHARD HAYWARD presents
FOR THE FIRST TIME ON ANY STAGE:

CASTLEREAGH

AN ULSTER PLAY OF 1798
By THOMAS CARNDUFF
(Author of "Workers," etc.)

A Play of Old Belfast in the Days of
HENRY JOY McCRACKEN

BEAUTIFULLY DRESSED IN AUTHENTIC COSTUMES OF THE PERIOD FROM
ONE OF THE WORLD'S MOST CELEBRATED WARDROBES.

THE CAST INCLUDES:
RICHARD HAYWARD   ELMA HAYWARD
CHARLES FAGAN   NANCY CULLEN
R. H. McCANDLESS   MYRTLE ADAMS
HAROLD GOLDBLATT
CHARLES E. OWENS
RAYMOND THOMPSON
R. FORSYTHE BOYD
BRUCE DAWSON

J. R. MAGEEAN, Producer.   Stage Direction: DAN FITZPATRICK.

NO INCREASE IN PRICES
Stalls 2/4. Back Stalls 1/6. Circle 1/3
All Numbered and Reserved.
BOOKING AT THE THEATRE 11 a.m. till 8-30 p.m.   TELEPHONE: BELFAST 3166.

Amateur Drama Festivals were held annually at the Empire with productions like the Rosario Players in *The Auction at Killybuck*, and Richard Hayward's Belfast Repertory Theatre in plays by Thomas Carnduff, the first shipyard dramatist.

Griffiths Knight tried to form a Little Theatre in the Ulster Minor Hall. After a year he was succeeded by Harold Norway who re-named it The Playhouse. But both failed to compete with the successful sound cinemas.

Even the Second World War and two German air raids had no effect on the Belfast cinemas. There were thousands of service personnel in Belfast and even more people trying to get into the picture houses. Travel restrictions between Great Britain and Northern Ireland stopped the touring companies and the variety artistes who appeared at the Belfast theatres.

46

Belfast News-Letter

MONDAY, SEPTEMBER 4, 1939

THEATRES, CINEMAS, ENTERTAINMENTS, &c.

NOTICE TO THE PUBLIC
CINEMAS & THEATRES

THE GOVERNMENT OF NORTHERN IRELAND do not consider it necessary at present to apply the Order closing Cinemas and Theatres to Northern Ireland. ALL CINEMAS AND THEATRES WILL, THEREFORE, REMAIN **OPEN** AND PROGRAMMES WILL BE SHOWN AS USUAL.

ISSUED BY THE AMUSEMENT CATERERS' ASSOCIATION, N.I.

HIPPODROME
CONRAD   VALERIE   SEBASTIAN
VEIDT   HOBSON   SHAW
in   "THE SPY IN BLACK"
ALSO
EDITH   CLIFF   RICHARD
FELLOWS EDWARDS FISKE
in "THE LITTLE ADVENTURESS"

TROXY   TO-DAY,
Tues. & Wed.
WALLACE BEERY & ROBERT TAYLOR
in "STAND UP AND FIGHT"
Showing at 2-45, 4-50, 6-55, 9-5.

EXCURSIONS, TOURS, &c.

L M S
NORTHERN COUNTIES
COMMITTEE

WITHDRAWAL.

OPERA HOUSE   6-40 Twice Nightly 8-50
CARL F. CLOPET (In association with PHILIP YORKE Productions, Ltd.)
Presents for the First Time in Belfast,
THE BIGGEST SUCCESS OF LONDON FOR FIFTY YEARS:
"FRENCH WITHOUT TEARS"
By TERENCE RATTIGAN
Box Office 10—10.   BOOK NOW!   'Phones: 22905 & 21845

ROYAL CINEMA
(ARTHUR SQUARE)
CONTINUOUS DAILY FROM 12-55 P.M.
ROBERT   REGINALD   ROSALIND   RALPH
MONTGOMERY   OWEN   RUSSELL   MORGAN
IN THE COMEDY MURDER MYSTERY
FAST AND LOOSE
(A METRO-GOLDWYN-MAYER PICTURE)
GRACIE FIELDS in "LOOK UP AND LAUGH"

Although the cinemas and theatres were not closed during the war, they did have problems. In July 1941, the Northern Ireland Amusement Caterers complained bitterly that the passport authorities in Great Britain would not allow 'artists of British nationality and over military age' to come to Northern Ireland to carry out their contracts. For the first time in almost half a century, the Opera House was unable to stage a Christmas pantomime.

Wartime theatres did have to be prepared for air raids, as this Empire programme cover shows.

PROGRAMME

WEEK COMMENCING MONDAY, 21st MAY, 1945
ONCE NIGHTLY AT 7.30
(Saturday 6.15 and 8.30)

"G" DISTRICT BELFAST CIVIL DEFENCE Presents:

"THE SIX SHOWS"

(Proceeds in aid of Civil Defence Benevolent Fund and Royal Victoria and Mater Hospital Bed Fund)

Monday, 21st May—7.30
HARLAND & WOLFF'S " SHIPYARD SHOW"
Guest Artistes: JIMMY O'DEA & CO.

Tuesday, 22nd May—7.30
SHORT & HARLAND'S "FLIGHT AMONG THE STARS"

Wednesday, 23rd May—7.30
THE MACKIE PLAYERS in "THE NEW GOSSOON"

Thursday, 24th May—7.30
CIVIL DEFENCE SERVICES' "EMPIRE DAY REVUE"
Guest Artiste: JIMMY O'DEA

Friday, 25th May—7.30
BELFAST COLLAR COMPANY'S "FAULAT ON PARADE"

Saturday, 26th May—6.15 and 8.30
TO END THE WEEK "THE HEADLINES AGAIN"

Front Stalls and Circle, 4/-; Back Stalls, 3/-; Gallery, 1/6.
(Including Tax)
BOOKING OFFICE, EMPIRE THEATRE, 11 to 7 p.m. Phone 24833.

Will Patrons Please Note, the Theatre will be
CLOSED all Next Week
Re-opening Monday, 4th June
WITH AN
...NTIRELY NEW EDITION
...ECORD-BREAKING REVUE
...THE SHOW"
...New Comedy and New Faces!

...is Week, 11 a.m. to 7 p.m. Next Week,
...a.m. till 4.30 p.m.

EMPIRE

"The most comfortable Theatre in Ulster"
Proprietors . . . . . The Belfast Empire Theatre of Varieties Ltd.
General Manager . . . . Gerald Morrison.

ONCE NIGHTLY at 7-30
(SATURDAYS & HOLIDAYS AT 6-20 & 8-30)

PROGRAMME

21/5/1945

PRICE THREEPENCE
BOX OFFICE OPEN DAILY 11 A.M. TILL 7 P.M.
PHONE 24833

A.R.P.
NOTICE TO OUR PATRONS.
You will be notified by a red warning light on each side of the proscenium if an Air Raid Warning has been given during the performance. This does not necessarily mean an air raid is taking place. If you wish to leave the theatre, you are at liberty to do so; but if you must go, all we ask is that you depart quietly and without excitement.
WE RECOMMEND YOU TO REMAIN IN THE THEATRE.

WEEK COMMENCING MONDAY, 5th JULY, 1943.

COME TO THE SHOW

100th EDITION

The Revue that has broken all Theatrical Records!

CAST:—BERT LENA, KATHLEEN & PAT McKAY, JACK OSBORNE, ANNA CRAWLEY, BILLY STUTT, SHEILA DALY, LOU CHARLESWORTH, JOE CAREY, ALASTAIR DICK, FREDDIE SALES & NORMA BARRY. With Our Girls—RENEE, NORAH, MOLLY, MAY, BILLIE, BLONDIE, VIOLET, TESSIE, ANNE & PHYLLIS.

GUEST ARTISTES:

JOSEPH McLAUGHLAN   JIM HAWTHORNE
JIMMY STEEN   BOBBIE GRAHAM   MOLLIE MILLAR

Scenes arranged by PAT McKAY
Dance ensembles by NORMA BARRY.
The Show Produced by GERALD MORRISON.

SCENE 1—"COME TO THE SHOW!"
SCENE 2—"THE ORACLE" .... BERT, FREDDIE & LOU
SCENE 3—MOLLIE MILLAR
SCENE 4—"INVITATION TO THE WALTZ"
SCENE 5—JIM HAWTHORNE
SCENE 6—"MICHAEL DOOLEY'S HOOLEY"
    SPECIAL BROADCAST EDITION by THE COMPANY

Intermission:

LESLIE BERESFORD & HIS EMPIRE ORCHESTRA

SCENE 7—"BATHING BELLES—Yesterday and To-day"
    ALASTAIR, NORMA, SHEILA & THE GLAMOURETTES
SCENE 8—"LADS OF THE VILLAGE"
    JACK, FREDDIE & BERT
SCENE 9—"FROM THE VERY MOMENT THAT WE MET"
The Prize-winning Song in the All-Ireland Song-writing Contest.
    Sung by ANNA CRAWLEY.
Accompanied on stage by the Composer, ELIZABETH QUINN.
SCENE 10—FREDDIE SALES
SCENE 11—MUSICAL COMEDY MEMORIES (No. 54)
    THE COMPANY
SCENE 12—JIMMY STEEN—Ulster's Own Comedian
SCENE 13—SHEILA DALY
SCENE 14—"WHAT'S YOURS,"
    BERT, FREDDIE, JACK, LOU & NORMA
SCENE 15—BILLY STUTT
SCENE 16—JOSEPH McLAUGHLAN
SCENE 17—GRAND FINALE—"LIGHTS UP!"
    JOSEPH McLAUGHLAN AND THE ENTIRE COMPANY

Programme Subject to Alteration.

GALA PERFORMANCE ON THURSDAY, 8th JULY, AT 6.40
Under the Distinguished Patronage of Their Graces The Duke and Duchess of Abercorn; The Rt. Hon. The Prime Minister (Sir Basil Brooke, Bart.) and Lady Brooke; The Rt. Hon. The Lord Mayor (Sir Crawford McCullagh, Bart.), etc.
Entire Proceeds to the Governor's Fund for the Red Cross and all War Charities.

Programme for the 100th edition of the Empire's wartime resident revue. Among the guest artistes note one Joseph McLaughlan, later to star under the name of Josef Locke.

The Grand Opera House had a stock company at that time – the Savoy Players. For six years they presented a different play each week and drew good audiences. Among the players were Guy Rolfe, later to go into films, Basil Lord, Jane Aird, Norman Chidgey, Maurice Maxwell, Evelyn Kerry, Jean Hamilton and Sheila Managhan.

Guy Luther Birch became the new proprietor at the Royal Hippodrome. He presented seasons of variety and revue as well as films. One original production was called *Play-Vaudi-Band*. It was a long show consisting of Sean O'Casey's *Juno and the Paycock*, an hour of variety artistes from Dublin, and a jazz band conducted by Peggy Dell. Strangely enough this odd mixture was very well received.

The Empire Theatre manager, Gerald Morrison, produced a residential musical revue called *Come to the Show* which ran successfully for six years. The performers were local artistes and entertainers from Dublin, and there was a change of programme each week.

But the greatest local theatrical enterprise was the Ulster Group Theatre, formed in 1939 from three amateur societies: the Carrickfergus Players, the North Irish Players and the Jewish Institute Players. They used the Ulster Minor Hall for performances, and Harold Goldblatt, R.H. McCandless and James Mageean between them produced the best Irish plays, alternating them with classical drama and successful plays from

LEGACY OF DELIGHT

A FARCICAL TRAGIC-COMEDY
BY HUGH QUINN

▼

CHARACTERS

David McFall	*Late of Sardinia Street Shankill Road, Belfast*	R. H. MacCandless
Martha McFall	*now of Derrygowan House.*	Min Milligan
Margaret McFall, *their daughter*		Magdalaine Johnson
Liza Jane McBey	*old neighbours of*	Jean Barrie
Alfie McCann	*the McFalls*	Joseph Tomelty
Watson, *the butler*		J. Kenneth Hamilton
Mr. Morell	*Guests at*	Alfred Arnold
Mrs. Morell	*the Garden Party*	Gertrude Duffin
Boy	*Derrygowan*	Louis Gilbert
Girl	*House*	Jean Lloyd
Mr. Cassel de Windt	*Guests at 2 Larkwood Villas*	Walter Brown
Mrs. Cassel de Windt		Jill Ballintyne
Mr. Pim, *a debt collector*		John McDade
Woman Customer		Rose Campbell

Would patrons please make a point of taking their seats before the curtain rises.

SCENES

ACT I

Reception Room, Derrygowan House,
Mid-day, July, 1936

ACT II

Scene I   The Dining Room, 2 Larkwood Villas,
7 p.m., Autumn, 1937

Scene II The Drawing Room, 2 Larkwood Villas,
continuous with Scene I

ACT III

Room behind the Shop, Sardinia Street,
Shankill Road, 8 p.m., Autumn, 1938

The Play produced by R. H. MacCandless

General Manager	Joseph Tomelty
Stage Manager	Dan Fitzpatrick
Electrician	Dan O'Connell

Sound Reproduction and Records by
W. Erskine Mayne.

There will be an INTERVAL of ten minutes between Acts II. and III. during which Tea may be obtained in the Foyer at moderate charges.

In 1943 the Group produced Hugh Quinn's 'Legacy of Delight', with many of Ulster's finest actors and producers. Young Louis Gilbert is there too, as a guest at the garden party.

other countries.

The Group was a huge success during the war years. For the first time, Ulster drama began to be taken seriously by producers, actors and — perhaps most importantly — audiences. New playwrights, such as John Montgomery, Hugh Quinn, and Joseph Tomelty were discovered. And many of the young actors who had their first chance on the boards at the Group were later to find fame on the London stage and in television. Names such as Lily Begley, Joseph Tomelty, James Ellis (Sergeant Lynch of *Z Cars*), Colin Blakely, J.G. Devlin and Harold Goldblatt.

Everyone in the Group was paid 30s, regardless of the size of his or her part. Rehearsal fees amounted to the princely sum of £1 — to cover *all* the rehearsing deemed necessary. Rehearsals were held on Sundays, but this was kept very quiet at the time, to avoid any controversy.

After the war there were changes: audiences were smaller in the theatres, though the cinemas still attracted people, with their new wide screens, bigger productions and realistic colour. The Royal Hippodrome reverted to films; the Opera House, unable to meet the expenses of touring companies, began showing films too, though the Empire continued with live shows. Seasons of resident revue and variety were alternated with drama and circuses.

But drama could still be successful. The first production of Sam Thompson's controversial play *Over the*

'Derek' meets a real window-cleaner in the corridors of Broadcasting House.

Bridge broke all box-office records at the Empire.

Thompson's play changed the Ulster Group Theatre completely. It had originally been accepted by them but the Belfast Corporation, who were subsidising the theatre, insisted on cuts in the script. The author refused to make them, and withdrew the play, which was then staged at the Empire, before going on tour around the Province. James Young took over at the Group, presenting farces and Ulster comedies written specially for him. Jimmy, as he was known to his fans, became a runaway success, helped by his popularity as 'Derek' the window-cleaner in *The McCooeys*.

A new theatre was built in Botanic Avenue. Hubert Wilmot and the Belfast Arts Theatre moved in to it, but overheads were high and to keep going, serious drama was replaced by farce and comedy. Plays by Sam Cree, like *Wedding Fever* and *Widow's Paradise*, became the mainstay of the theatre.

The Lyric Theatre had not yet moved into their purpose built premises in Ridgeway Street but were still producing some of the best Irish drama (in particular the works of W.B. Yeats) in very restricted conditions in the Derryvolgie Avenue house of Mary and Pearse O'Malley.

But the increasing popularity of television was bringing drastic changes to entertainment in Ulster by the mid Fifties. It was no longer necessary to go out to a cinema or a theatre. 'Talking pictures' were available at your own fireside and soon the old cinemas began to disappear, many of them converted into warehouses or stores. Others were demolished and are now almost forgotten. Even the large luxury cinemas erected in the 1930s to meet the talkie boom changed into supermarkets and furniture showrooms.

At the end of the 1950s there was an ominous rumour, later to become a reality, forecasting that the historic Empire Theatre was soon to be demolished. Without the singers, the dancers, and the comedians, Belfast's Victoria Square would never be quite the same. Perhaps the same is also true of the many districts, or 'villages' of Belfast, where for decades there was a wealth of cinema entertainment literally on your doorstep wherever you lived.

And sadly the old Picture House (or the Avenue as it has been more recently known), the first cinema to bring the 'talkies' to Belfast, has itself become the latest casualty of changing times. It closed its doors as a cinema on Saturday 23 October 1982.

EMPIRE THEATRE

Forthcoming Attractions :

NEXT WEEK—

'SANDY'S HERE AGAIN'

With SANDY DAW.

March 18th—

"Harlem Night Birds."

March 25th—

"Young and Beautiful."

April 1st—

"Meet us To-night."

April 8th—

Ella Shields and Variety.

Sam McAughtry

For many years Sam McAughtry was a civil servant. But he was also something else, and I'm glad to say still is. He is a man possessed with a keen and observant eye and with the ability to translate what he sees into his highly entertaining stories. Whenever I read them, or even better, when I hear Sam read them himself I always feel 'I wish I'd thought of that!' Born in the Tiger's Bay area of north Belfast, Sam had a tough upbringing, but there was always humour there too. And that humour was shared by many of the sports stars of yesteryear, and by those who loyally supported them week by week, long before television brought it all into our homes.

When Soccer was Soccer..

Looking back over half a century of sporting recollections my main impression is of the lack of material reward offered to our stars. In these times the most moderate sporting achievement brings with it the promise of riches and security, but our heroes walked the cobbled streets in our midst, working for our own level of wages, and meeting and marrying exactly the same sort of people that they would have mixed with had they never kicked a ball, or knocked a man out in the ring.

A girl in our street went out with Soldier Jones, who played in the Irish national soccer side right through from 1930 until 1937, and in the famous Linfield Irish Cup winning sides of 1930, '31 and '34. It might be of interest to reflect on the compositon of the Blues' 1930 team, and to consider that when each game was over, the following Linfield legends tidied themselves up and got the tram home to a parlour or kitchen house, after entertaining tens of thousands of spectators: Lawson; Brown, Watson; McCleery, Jones and Sloan; Houston, McCracken, Bambrick, Grice and McCaw.

As I was saying, Soldier Jones went out with a girl from Cosgrave Street in Tiger's Bay when he was at the height of his fame, and behind the curtains the women of the street watched as he stood, a good-looking, loose-limbed athlete, fidgeting at the corner of Lilliput Street, going through the mill as he had never done on the soccer field, being drawn out of position and leaving his defences wide open to a pretty weaver in York Street Flax Spinning Company.

To reach the Irish international team was some achievement in those days. I'm talking about the days when the Grove Fields at Skegoneil could attract a crowd of 3,000 unemployed men to watch a couple of sides called Hillview and North Star, the latter named after the pub at the foot of Cosgrave Street which is still there to this day. The publican, Paddy McEldowney, bought the team a new rig and a local character called Kaiser Mawhinney pawned it before anybody had a chance to wear it.

When I was a kid of eight or nine only two teams mattered to me: they were Crusaders and Brantwood. Both sides played in the Intermediate League, and when they met at Seaview the tiny ground was jammed until it nearly burst, while those who hadn't even the sixpence admission money sat on a height on the other side of the Shore Road known as Biroo Hill and saw the game for nothing. The crack was better on Biroo Hill, for some reason, than it ever was in the ground.

From these sides we had heroes like Silver Gough and Shooter Flack – for don't forget those were the great days when men were true individuals, and specific nicknames were attached to them in order to emphasise their uniqueness. Sticky Sloan of the Blues might have had another forename, but not many of us could have rattled it off readily. Even Joe Bambrick's proper name developed into something special with the rise of the

SIX GOALS FOR BAMBRICK

WELSH SOCCER ROUT

BEATEN 7-0 AT PARADISE

LINFIELD CENTRE THE HERO

CROWD'S DELIRIOUS DELIGHT

(Photo: Lyttle.)
BAMBRICK.

It was Ireland's day out at Celtic Park this afternoon, and that with a team which had caused misgiving.

Wales started prominently, but when Bambrick, at the end of twelve minutes' play, opened the score a great change came over the game. True, Wales seemed to have better ball control, and their combination for a time was well nigh perfect. But a tenacious half-back line was equal to the occasion, and when just on the interval Bambrick registered his second goal the ultimate result did not seem to be in doubt.

The second half came as a revelation. Bambrick ran riot, and his

better fate than that the ball should crash into the upright.

The game terminated in a series of sensations, the rampant Bambrick scoring his sixth goal—the double hat trick—and

'Belfast Telegraph' report of Bambrick's feat (1 February 1930).

jingle: *Head, heel or toe: slip it to Joe!* He rammed in six goals against Wales in 1930, and of all the football heroes in Northern Ireland's history none has ever eclipsed Joe Bambrick over all the years: not even George Best, for when you get right down to it, in soccer goals are of the essence, or as modern commentators would put it, 'The game is about scoring goals.'

There was a sort of 'B' side to Joe Bambrick's feat, for one of our favourite quiz questions, sitting on the pavement of an evening, was 'Who scored the other goal when Bambrick scored his six?' The answer is that the man who made it 7–0 that day was McCluggage of Burnley, in case an old, doddering soccer fan should stop you in the street and ask.

Joe Bambrick (second from the left of the action) scoring a goal for Linfield against United in 1931.

Soccer's catchment area fifty years ago was huge. In our schools the game was vibrant, even palpitating. I had a brother who was out of work for a year after he left school; he was a useful player, and the headmaster of the elementary school that we attended paid our Mart half a crown a week out of his own pocket to train the school team. That's how important a place soccer had in school life. Schools international matches were watched by capacity crowds; even the schools selection games were capable of drawing three or four thousand to St Mary's Ground opposite Solitude on the Cliftonville Road.

My own school produced a schoolboy international — a magnificent player, with delicate ball control and a drive like a six-inch shell. He must, alas, be nameless, for he had one of the shortest careers in football ever known, being warned off for life after reaching the Irish League and an illustrious club. In our part of the world we played rough, tough football, and this poor chap just forgot himself for a wee minute. It was in our systems, the hard game. I remember my own surprise when, playing my first game for St Barnabas in the Church Lads' Brigade League, I was ordered off against St Columba's, Knock, for going over the ball. Until then, I'd never been told it was an infringement. I humped off calling the referee an oul' woman.

In the 1982 World Cup competition I was privileged to spend a fortnight with the newest legends in Northern Ireland football – the side that made it to Phase 2, and an honourable exit from the last twelve. In their HQ, the Sidi Saler Hotel just outside Valencia in Spain, I had the opportunity to study at close quarters the young men who have succeeded to the acclaim once earned by such as Bambrick, Sloan, Jones, Mahood, Geary, McCaw and that magnificent goalkeeper and character, Elisha Scott.

The modern young men are fitter and faster and much more amenable to discipline than my boyhood heroes. And in their lifestyles, because of their wealth, they are so far out of reach of such as Soldier Jones that he would probably touch his cap, should they, by some time-trick, meet in the same generation. But, because of the individual way in which they learned to play, the footballers of the Twenties and Thirties were immeasurably more entertaining, and I know that if they were to be brought back again today to play their inimitable styles of football at the Oval, or Windsor, or Celtic Park, then today's fans would flock to see them, and the roads that lead to the grounds would be jammed as they were then I was a boy. For fifty years ago it was football that was played, and not snakes and ladders.

When William wore Orange

When Dunmore Park opened towards the end of the 1920s the whole of North Belfast was buzzing. I remember somebody telling me that the new people who had bought the ground were going to introduce whippet racing.

'What's a whippet?' I wanted to know.

'How the hell do I know,' replied the other, 'but whatever they are they're going to race them here.'

Well, it wasn't whippets that were raced, but 'grues'. And Dunmore Stadium brought much more than sorely-needed work to the area. It introduced to us the hope of riches — well, maybe not exactly riches, but the chance of laying hands on a few quid, for the first time in our lives. When the stadium opened for business some of our Tiger's Bay men were on the staff. Kaiser Mawhinney walked One Red, and our Mart walked Two Blue, and Geek Ross was an odd-job-man about the place, and the streets where we lived were alive with rumours about betting coups.

One of my earliest recollections was of Kaiser Mawhinney walking a certain dog right out the Antrim Road the whole way to Ballyclare, in order to stop it that night.

Kaiser shoved his whole wage of thirty shillings on to one to beat the marathon dog. The neighbourhood of North Belfast, knowing Kaiser's abysmal gambling record, stood off and watched. And they were right. The grue that had walked to Ballyclare was out nearly before the lid of the trap opened. It travelled round the 525 yards in a brown blur, and finished so far ahead of the field that the other dogs must have thought they were running in a totally separate race. 'That dog's crooked,' Kaiser Mawhinney claimed. He wanted the race declared void, on the grounds that he had been led to believe that the winner had sore paws, but all he succeeded in doing was founding a new school of dog training, involving a walk to Ballyclare every day.

This and a hundred other stories like it were common currency in the gorgeous days when greyhound racing was brand new and exciting. There were tiny triumphs for so many of us, to brighten the lives of all concerned. I'll never forget the night our Jack followed the advice of a well-to-do customer on the Corporation bus that he conducted, and stuck a quid on a seven-to-one shot at Dunmore.

It won. Mother heard about it from an excited punter who rushed home ahead of Jack, and she put a new pinny on to greet the conquering hero. Jack gave her a quid, me and the other small McAughtrys a bob each, and went down to York Street next morning and bought a BSA bike, brand new, for £4.19.11. Stimulated by this, the other mothers in Tiger's Bay at once began to lean on their offspring to have a bit of a whale at the bow-wows. That shiny bicycle was visible proof of the possibilities.

The real memories of greyhound racing, of course, have to include the war years and later. Wherever doggie

Crowds packing the stands at Dunmore Stadium.

punters gather together names like Priceless Border and West Halt are bound to crop up. The latter was one of the biggest turn-ups in local greyhound racing history, when it won a heat of the National Sprint at 50–1 in the Forties. There were all the Myroe dogs, and the Farloe dogs; there was Saltbox Row and there was Buddley Up.

58

DUNMORE STADIUM 'COMING OF AGE' 1928-1949

Mr B. Hughe's "Benburb Abbey" leading Mrs S. T.M°Laughlin's "Coomacullan" (the winner) and Mr R. Smyth's "Blue Sheegaba" at the first hurdle

Mr R.D. Best handing over "The Coming of age" Cup to the owner of "Jungle Pine" Mr J.A. M°Kee is on left.

Group of competitors for "The coming of age" Cup

The owner of "Jungle Pine" winner of "The coming of age" Cup race

Mr J.A M°Kee cutting the Birthday cake with Mrs J. Spence Captain J. Ross Mr D. Campbell and Mr N. Booth.

There was a dog called William that came out in the late Forties just before the Twelfth, in racing colours of Six Orange. The whole track, Mick and Prod, was on it, and it won to the accompaniment of the loudest cheers ever heard at Dunmore Park.

At a guess it was around 1934 when the fabulous greyhound Mick the Miller went into retirement after winning the highest honours in English racing. They brought Mick the Miller to Dunmore Park for a solo exhibition run, and I was one of a crowd of kids peeking over the fence from the outside, as the record-breaking dog flew around the track. The local papers described him as a 'grey streak', as he made his historic run.

There was once a dog called Crimson Clown. It was very popular, and won money for the fans more than once. But early in the Thirties, Crimson Clown took a bad tumble at the bottom bend, and had to be destroyed. Today legend has it that Crimson Clown lies buried at that spot. The followers of the sport, more sentimental than you would think, would love to think that the legend has a basis in fact.

The years that have gone by since then have seen many changes in greyhound racing, not least the improvement in the reliability of breeding. For don't forget that racing pedigrees didn't go back along a very pure bloodstock line in those days. The people who interested themselves in the sport in Northern Ireland fifty years ago played their part in legitimising greyhound racing, and making of it a lucrative breeding industry, at least in the South, and these people deserve the best that history can bestow on them. There were breeders from Ballymena and Derry and Fermanagh in those early days who lost an awful lot of money by experiments, but who produced winning lines for both speed and stamina, and in doing so began the process that has culminated in the fine industry that exists all over Ireland today.

And in these times, when racing in the North is in decline, we should applaud those stalwarts who persevere in their efforts to make the sport as popular today as it was when I was a boy. A brave handful of sportsmen are underwriting the operations of Dunmore and Celtic Parks today, and they deserve all the support that they can get.

I would love to see again the days when the whole area around the stadium was black with customers in the minutes before the racing began; when we kids made a few bob minding taxis and cars outside, and kept our fingers crossed that our big brothers who were punting inside the track, would 'clear the card' and, just for a day or so, bring a magic carpet home to the cramped and hungry streets of Belfast.

DOGS IN TRAMS

Sir—Once again "The Roamer" draws attention to dogs on tram-cars and trolleybuses, creating the altogether erroneous impression that dogs are constantly and regularly monopolising seating accommodation on these vehicles. He quotes what must be a rare instance of an owner with two greyhounds taking up seating, and of two ladies apparently forced hurriedly to leave the 'bus. This is an unusual incident, and as a result of inquiries in a general way I am informed by an official that complaints about dogs—large dogs especially—travelling on trams and 'buses are rare.

Even on race evening, when reasonable facilities for greyhounds to travel to the meetings are expected, few of these animals are noticed, and owners seem to be extremely careful that no offence or annoyance is caused to passengers.

The greyhound is now a sporting pastime of a section of the community unable to afford the ownership of racehorses or motor cars; so why should they suffer or be penalised by comments likely to arouse antagonism?—Yours, &c.,

DOGS IN TRAMS

Sir—With reference to Mr. Dalzell's letter in to-day's issue it may be inferred that he does not live on any of the tram routes leading to dog-racing. I would suggest to him that if a man can afford to keep racing dogs he can quite well bear the expense of a private motor car or taxi. Let the trams be used solely for their legitimate purpose. Thank you, "Roamer."—Yours, &c., August 10, 1945. ROVER.

Sir—I have great respect for Mr. Alexander Dalzell as an authority on dogs, but I cannot agree with him that owners of greyhounds should be allowed to use public service vehicles as travelling kennels.—Yours, &c. DOG LOVER. August. 10, 1945.

The Greatest Show on Earth

My final recollection of sport over the last fifty years concerns my favourite people – the pugilists. I had a cousin who took up the game in 1938. He trained in a kitchen house in Conlon Street converted for the purpose, and he got ten bob for six rounds from Ma Copley, the redoubtable lady who ran the Chapel Fields in Alfred Street. When he graduated to eight-rounders he got a pound, out of which his trainer got half a crown and his trainer's brother another half crown, because the trainer's brother pestered until he was paid. The cousin gave his mother ten bob, and then he and I would sit in the chippy and eat fish suppers. Next morning he would wake up with black eyes and more, and maybe three bob to show for his pains.

There were so many boxing stadiums in Belfast that we were spoiled for choice. And there were boxers in plenty to fill them. Tommy Stewart from York Street was a favourite in the lighter divisions, as was Jim McStravick, a delightful flyweight. Later his younger brother Terry was to bring the Province closer to world renown in the 10–11 stone reaches than anyone in history, but he chucked the game just when he was at his best. Barney Wilson from the markets, a punishing body-puncher, thought he was the best until in 1939 he met Tommy Armour. The referee stopped it in seven, after Wilson had sampled the hardest left hook ever to be bred in Ireland. Indeed, so severe was Armour's dig that he put Eric Boon, the British lightweight champion, to bye-byes in Belfast,

one day in 1943 when Boon was rash enough to mix it in the corner.

We had Patsy Quinn and Gerry McCready and Spike McCormick and Jimmy Ingle and Chuck Flannigan in the welter division, and these were scrappers who weren't afraid to fight often. By the time Tommy Armour retired he had fought over 180 fights, knocked out forty opponents, and finished another forty inside the distance. He won thirteen out of his first fourteen fights in 1936, all of them by the short route. Nowadays, if that were to happen, there'd be a syndicate of millionaires camping out on the boxer's doorstep, waiting to make him a superstar. In Armour's case, the victories upped his money to £2 a fight.

There was Dan McCallister, and there was Spider Kelly, both boxing masters. When Spider won the British featherweight title in 1937 we went stone mad. Nearly every night in the season there was a boxing bill on somewhere in the Province, never mind the Harps Hall and the Ring in Thomas Street and the Chapel Fields and the Ulster Hall in Belfast. Billy Meharg, the York Street Thunderer, was a great favourite, as was the Shankill Road bantam, Jackie Musson.

But for my money the greatest light ever to shine on Irish boxing – brighter even that the lustre shed by the gifted Rinty Monaghan, world flyweight champion – was that provided by the talents of Jimmy Warnock. He was a shy introvert who, in the fashion of the time in

Boxer Rinty Monaghan training on Cavehill for his fight with Dan Marino (1947).

Ireland, was badly managed. But at his best he beat the great Benny Lynch in 1936 in Belfast, and again the following year in Glasgow, Lynch's home town. And the British couldn't take it. They denied Warnock a world title chance, until his poor handling and personal approach to the game guaranteed that Ireland would not gain a world champion at that particular time.

Warnock's first fight was in 1931. He won KO2. In his first sixteen scraps he lost only one. His record, by the time 1935 arrived, was like a roll-call of the cream of world flyweight talent, and the world just then, unlike the post-war years, was bursting with talent. Tut Whalley, Maurice Huguenin, Tiny Bostock, Benny Lynch – he beat them all. In 1937 he beat Katsumi Morioka, Etienne Ferraro, and Benny Lynch again, but this was as far as he went. From then on it was downhill. Peter Kane stopped him in an eliminator for the world title in August 1937, and the light was spent. Warnock fought again many times afterwards, but for those of us who worshipped him, the spectacle was distressing.

In those far-off days we all fancied ourselves at the scrapping. There were boxing clubs everywhere. We had boxing on the brain. Isn't it a funny thing that we could walk the streets unmolested? It was only when boxing began to die out amongst the working-class kids that brutality started to stalk the streets.

In my glance back down the years I have focussed on only three sports. There were others, of course, but soccer, greyhound racing, and boxing were the main sporting preoccupations of the working-class people fifty years ago. The people who reached the top in sport in those days climbed far higher mountains to get there than today's petulant prima donnas could manage, and my boyhood heroes got little more than fame for reward. They were exploited, sometimes cruelly, but they loved the sports that they graced.

In times that were very hard indeed, the footballers and the boxers lifted us out of cold reality. For only a few coppers we were given what seemed to us the greatest show on earth. Then, afterwards, these magnificent performers threw on their coats and joined us once again in the cramped streets. Thus, in every possible way, they were our own superstars. That's why they are remembered so clearly today, when so many postwar sporting figures are forgotten.

Tom McDevitte

Tom McDevitte worked on the railways for many years. But perhaps 'work' is the wrong way to think about it because it was much more of a love affair. There are very few corners of the Province where you can't see signs of some of the the old railway lines which criss-crossed the Province in the days when steam was king. In some cases it's been a long time since the sight and sound of these branch lines was a reality, but Tom can bring them back to mind instantly because that is where he finds the inspiration for his railway yarns. And just as important as the places are the people, the characters who travelled on the trains and those who worked as 'servants' of the railway companies. But Tom has also been a traveller in a more energetic sense and has cycled the length and breadth of Ireland. And he loves to tell today's listeners of those memories from the past too. For the past forty years and more Tom has been known as the popular country character 'Barney McCool of Coolaghey' on both radio and television, and for over twenty years has been writing a weekly column in the 'Tyrone Constitution', a column which is read world-wide to judge from the letters he receives from Irish 'exiles' delighted to hear a bit of crack.

Transports of Delight

The railway station in my native town of Strabane was a joint one, that is, it served both the broad-gauge Great Northern Railway and the narrow-gauge County Donegal lines, which ran to, amongst other places, Letterkenny and Ballybofey.

To avoid the risk of accidents, a footbridge spanned all the tracks, and a man was stationed at the Great Northern platform with strict instructions to ensure that all passengers used it. This was to be by means of a long and wordy recitation which he in his wisdom reduced to 'Over the bridge to Ballybofey'.

One day a 'little old lady, dressed in lace' – a complete stranger – approached him with the intention of asking for assistance with her trunk, still in the guard's van: 'Porter! I have a tin chest in— '

'A tin chest!' he roared. 'I don't care if you have a wooden leg – ye still go over the bridge to Ballybofey!'

The line to Letterkenny crossed the Border into the (then) Irish Free State at Lifford and after wending its way casually past places such as Raphoe and Convoy, climbed up the Cornagillagh bank (hills are always banks to railwaymen) and eventually rolled down into Letterkenny. In the process it passed by a little townland (not even a village) called Pluck which was given a sense of importance far beyond its size when some 'returned Yank', boasting of his travels, would be brought down to earth by a sarcastic native saying, 'Ach – houl' yer tongue man – were ye ever in Pluck?'

During the 1939 war years – or the Emergency as it was called in the Free State – hundreds of wagon loads of turf from Donegal passed over that line to Strabane and thence to Dublin to 'keep the home fires burning' in the capital.

One such train-load was standing at Letterkenny Station one day, and I got a lift on the engine to Strabane, in return for shovelling coal into the firebox.

As we were moving 'with laboured step and slow' – very very slow – up Cornagillagh bank, I paused in my shovelling, stuck my head out of the side of the engine cab to gasp some fresh air, and in so doing I noticed away at the back of the thirty-seventh and last wagon of turf, a little white butterfly fluttering alongside. Believe it or not, it gradually overtook the train, and came to rest on the coal behind the engine. In other words the butterfly was flying faster than the train! After resting for a time, it flew on to the front of the engine, rested another while on the boiler, but eventually it gave up and flew on ahead by itself. It must have been in a hurry!

Laugh if you like, but it's true!

Another narrow-gauge railway ran from Londonderry through Letterkenny through wild and rocky country to the little fishing port of Burtonport on the western seaboard of Donegal – a long slow five or six hour's journey on the timetable, and even longer and slower in reality.

An American was doing this journey once and by the

time he reached Barnes Gap, a rocky defile almost devoid of any vegetation, he was already almost a 'lifetime friend' of the Guard. You can imagine the Guard's surprise when on looking out of his van he espied the American away up on the top of the rocky cutting.

'Hi! Aren't you supposed to be a passenger on this train?' he shouted.

'Sure am!' replied the Yank.

'Well what are ye doin' up thonder?'

'Picking flowers,' said he.

'Flowers? Sure there's no flowers up there.'

'I know,' said he, 'but I've a packet of seeds with me!'

No wonder the Londonderry & Lough Swilly Railway was dubbed the Late, Lazy and Slow Railway.

The Permanent way was anything but permanent – the engines rolled like a ship at sea and the passengers were thrown about like peas in a drum. Once, however, for about a mile or so the track had been re-laid because of flooding, and it was so smooth that one young fireman yelled to his driver, 'Jump, Jimmy, jump! She must be on the sleepers!'

A relief booking-clerk once found himself in a pickle when asked for a ticket to 'Crew'. In reality this was a station on the roadside tramway which ran from Victoria Bridge to Castlederg and not the famous junction in England.

Drawing himself up to his full five and a half feet of pomposity, the clerk looked through the small window at this 'country gam' and said, 'You want a ticket to Crewe? Saloon or steerage? Via Liverpool or Heysham?'

The countryman, not understanding one word, could only gasp in open-mouthed astonishment. 'W-w-what?'

'I asked you if you wanted to travel saloon or steerage and by which route, Liverpool or Heysham!'

His pomposity was soon deflated when he got the answer: 'Ach away and have a titter o' wit. I'm goin' by Victoria Bridge.'

'The Mail' was the train of the day, stopping only at the principal stations between Londonderry and Belfast, and

This is an age of speed, no doubt, as you will all agree.
You can fly to America twice as quick as you can sail the sea.
But you may talk about your aeroplanes and ships that sail the Main
Why, man-a-dear they wouldn't get near the Letterkenny Train

When she pulls out from Strabane you will hear the porters shout:
'Get ready for the Customs, for at Lifford they'll take ye out
And when you get to that big town you show them all your bags
And if you don't be nice to the Customs men they'll leave you there – in rags!

Away from Lifford she will go and fly through Ballindrait
Till she pulls up in Raphoe – just half an hour late.
But if you want to have a drop in Coolaghy, of radio fame,
Just ask the Guard for him to stop the Letterkenny Train.

She leaves the mills of Convoy in a powerful cloud of steam
And climbs through Cornagillagh and on to Glenmaquin
And that's where all the tourists get out to have a look
At that very important city that goes by the name of Pluck!

Then down the hill the train flies fast to Letterkenny town,
And birds and butterflies fly past, turn back, and circle round.
It's mentioned in the Bible – it's all writ down quite plain
Where the Lord He made all creeping things – the Letterkenny train!

The 'Great Vic' – 'a terminal with atmosphere' the 'Belfast Telegraph' called it when they printed this picture. Before the Central Station was built, this was Belfast's main station.

sometimes, at speed, picking up mail bags which had been suspended on special fittings at certain stations.

This train ran non-stop from Omagh to Dungannon, and was followed almost immediately by another train which stopped at all the intermediate stations, such as Beragh and Sixmilecross.

It so happened that a 'wee woman from Beragh' was shopping in Omagh, and rushing up to the train she saw steaming at Omagh station, she jumped into it as it was leaving, sat down gasping and then as it approached her station, Beragh, she gathered up all her parcels, opened the door, and stepped out!

Unknown to her it was the Non-stop Mail and had only slowed to pick up the 'Staff'!

In the words of a local, 'Man sorr – if ye'd a seen the pant! She opened the door and stepped out – aye and the train doing a mile a square minit at the time – and ploughed a trench a yard wide up the length of the platform, smashed through a palin' and rolled down the bank and intil an oul sheugh – up till her oxters in clabber!

'The Stationmaster foamed for a heerse and got a bag and a shovel and ran over to gather her up – but ye'll never believe it! Sowl boy wasn't she sittin' up in the sheugh, wipin' the glar from in under her oxters, and fixin' the oul' straw hat wi' the wax berries on it, and says the Stationmaster, "Ach Maggie dear – are ye kilt?"

"Not a bit of it," says she, "but sowl boy that train didn't stap long here the day!"'

Just a few miles across the country from there is the small town of Fintona, which was connected to the main Derry–Enniskillen railway line about a mile away by a horse tramway, which lasted for 104 years.

The tram itself was similar to the old horse-trams in Belfast: First and Second Class passengers inside – and Third Class on top. Supposed to hold twenty inside and thirty on top, it often carried anything up to a hundred, including those standing on the front beside the driver, those hanging on to the back, and those hanging on to those on top! It has been featured many times in the Press, on Radio and Television, and truly is known world wide.

All the horses were called Dick – but truth to tell they weren't horses at all, but mares! They were so well used to the timetables that after being unhooked at Fintona, they would wander over to their stable but be certain to come out in time for the next trip and stand beside the tram ready to be hooked up again. Indeed somebody said that if you held up your ticket to 'Dick', he would have nipped it for you!

It closed down on 30 September 1957, and was later taken to the Transport Museum, Witham Street, Belfast, where it still stands – minus the horse, of course! – for all to see.

THE FINTONA VAN

You have read about the chariots of Egypt,
  Of the slide cars and the slipes of olden time:
Of the cruel car of Juggernaut from India
  And the rickshaws of an Oriental clime.

Now the vehicle I write about is older,
  Though its origin for ages was kept dark,
For the van they call the railway van at Fintona
  Is constructed from the remnants of the Ark.

The directors who control its every movement,
  Know its value as an antique to a "make,"
And its speed must not exceed that of a funeral,
  Lest its Gopher constitution gets a shake.

Since there are so few attractions in the village,
  I'm sure the van supplies a long-felt want,
For of creeping things that creepeth on this planet,
  'Tis the very rarest specimen extant.

68

The Fintona tram (or van, as it was known locally).

G. N. R. (Ireland)
Issued subject to the conditions & regulations
in the Co's Time Tables, Books Bills & Notices
NOT TRANSFERABLE
Third Class Fare 0s 1d
Fintona TO
FINTONA JUNCTION
III FintonaJ.

106

Wouldn't it be strange if someone hadn't made up a poem about it? And that's what the late Mat Mulcaghey (the 'Oul Besom Man from Tyrone') who in reality was Wilson Guy, the local creamery manager, just did.

One of the most famous of all Irish tramways or roadside railways was the Clogher Valley which for 37½ miles ran from the Great Northern Station at Tynan in Co. Armagh, through the towns of Aughnacloy, Ballygawley, Augher, Clogher and Fivemiletown in Tyrone, to connect with the Great Northern again at Maguiresbridge in Co. Fermanagh.

The stations were all substantial redbrick buildings but the halts along the roadside, such as Aghnahilla, Farranetra, Tattyknuckle and the like, were just a nameplate hung on the hedge. As a man said, 'Two barrels and a plank and ye tuk them in at night out of the rain!'

The tram would have got no prizes for speeding – as an old ballad said:

Our express we cannot lose – it's safer nor a pram,
Sure it goes three miles in half an hour,
The Clogher Valley tram.

In fact I once heard that at Tynan Station, the Great Northern train was being delayed awaiting the connection and the Stationmaster, well noted for his hasty temper, shouted:

The Clogher Valley Railway passing through the centre of Fivemiletown. Note the ornamental clock to the right of the photograph.

'Where the so-and-so is that so-and-so oul hearse of a tram?'

Just then a dog was seen running up the hill towards the station and a Porter replied, 'She can't be far away now, Sir. Sure there's the driver's dog and he always runs on ahead of her!'

As well as running alongside the hedge of the country road and occasionally disappearing through the hedge to make short-cuts at a bend in the road, it steamed up the middle of the main street of Fivemiletown, and underneath the clock in its ornamental frame which was

erected to commemorate the Coronation of King Edward VII in 1903, and which incidentally is still in place. Of course the clock occasionally needed attention and once when it stopped altogether a man came out from Enniskillen to effect repairs. In an endeavour to diagnose the trouble he said, 'So she's stopped, has she? Tell me this now, when did she start to stop?'

A commercial traveller from Londonderry doing business in Fivemiletown had to chase down the street after the 'tram' to try to get to his next port of call, Augher. Eventually he managed to grab the buffers and hauled himself up on to them and sat there, stridelegs for a mile or so until the 'tram' stopped alongside the road for another passenger.

That's when the Guard saw this man sitting on the buffers and before he could get down, the Guard raised a ruction and reported him to the General Manager for 'riding on an unauthorised part of the train and without a ticket forbye'!

Round about the turn of the century you could have got a cheap day return ticket to Armagh for 1/8d or to Belfast for 4/6d or even on special occasions through to Bangor for 5/6d, changing of course into the GNR train at Tynan. But surely the most wonderful trip of all was on August Bank Holiday 1890 when they advertised: 'The trip of the Season! To Enniskillen via Maguiresbridge by rail and a cruise as far as Castlecaldwell and back on one of the First Class Steamers of the Royal Erne Navy. All for 5/- from Aughnacloy.'

CLOGHER VALLEY RAILWAY
Diesel Rail Coach Service

SUMMER
TIME TABLE

FIRST-CLASS TRAVEL AT
THIRD-CLASS FARE   ::

For further particulars apply to—
D. N. McCLURE,
GENERAL MANAGER,
AUGHNACLOY.

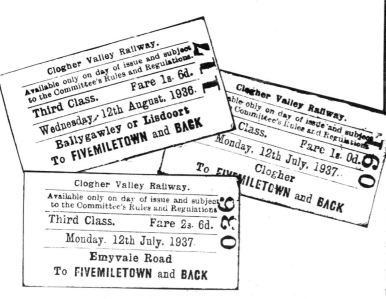

Despite all the special offers, however, it made a loss year after year, until eventually on the last day of December, 1941, the last train ran. It was sold, largely for scrap for use in the war effort; that is, for conversion into bombs, shells and battleships, and this prompted a local bank manager to write its epitaph in the form of the thoughts of an old countryman.

ENTERPRISE *a* **GNR**

NON-STOP EXPRESS

And so passed into oblivion, gone but certainly not forgotten, the Clogher Valley Railway of 'glorious and immortal memory'.

They tuk our oul railway away, so they did,
And sowl the whole lot for a few thousand quid.
They say the ratepayers here are well rid –
Ach, ahmdambut boys, it's tarrah!

For fifty long years she puffed to and fro,
At times she'd get there; at other times no;
She's worth more dead than alive, so must go –
Ach, ahmdambut boys, it's tarrah!

She ran down back gardens and up the Main street
And frightened the horses she happen to meet,
And now she's tuk aff for to build up the fleet –
Ach, ahmdambut boys, it's tarrah!

I hear they're for sellin' the oul line for scrap
For to make into bombs for to plaster the map,
Well, here's hopin' oul Hitler's below when they drap –
Ach, ahmdambut boys, it's tarrah!

They say that the Air Force soon will begin
To use up our Railway, this war for to win;
They'll drap Clogher Station all over Berlin!
Ach, ahmdambut boys, it's tarrah!

Them Nazis now boast of a new submarine,
They say it's the finest that ever was seen;
A CVR depth charge will leave it 'has been' –
Ach, ahmdambut boys, it's tarrah!

When the Roosians and us march down Wilhelmstrasse
Oul Hitler'll say: 'Boys, but I'm the quare ass –
Sure I might have knowed Clogher could still houl the
pass.
Ich dambut boys – it's tarrah!'

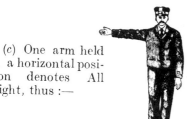

(c) One arm held in a horizontal position denotes All Right, thus :—

All Right Signal.

51. *In the absence of Flags—*

(a) Both arms raised above the head denotes Danger, thus :—

Danger Signal.

(b) One arm raised above the head denotes Caution, thus :—

Caution Signal.

VOL. XXXIII. No. II   NOVEMBER 1948

MECCANO
MAGAZINE

ENTERPRISE

N° 84

LEAVING BELFAST

6D.

The Big Day Out

by Bill Nesbitt

I've travelled this weary world of ours by land, and air, and
    sea,
And I think that I've seen about everything that's ever
appealed to me –
Exotic sights, like the Northern Lights, or the jungles of
    Brazil,
Or the Taj Mahal by moonlight – and I marvel at them still.

Yet, wherever I have wandered, or no matter where I've
    been,
And in spite of all the things I've done, or all the sights I've
    seen,
I swear that there is nothing that gave me such great joy
As when I went to Bangor on the steam-train, as a boy.

I remember the excitement, and the sheer exhilaration
As I clutched my pennies in my hand and went down to the
    station,
And the special smell of burning coal was magic in the air
To an innocent wee fellow who didn't have a care.

Then, when the train got started, and chugged along the
    track,
I'd open up the window, my face all sooty black,
And I'd look up to the engine, to try to see it flame –
And I'd see a hundred little boys doing just the same.

I remember, when I got there, the skies were blue and bright,
The sun was always shining, the temperature just right,
And I'd head at once for Pickie, and splash about the pool
With my shoulders getting sun-tanned, and the water nice
    and cool.

And when I'd finished swimming, I'd head down to the
    shore
And I'd hunt the pools for shrimps and crabs, and catch
    them
by the score;
After that, I'd go and buy a 'slider' or a 'poke'
(For in those days we hadn't heard of hamburgers or Coke!).

I'd try to skim a stone or two on every seventh wave.
And at last I'd head for Barry's, a real Aladdin's cave,
And there I'd look about me, my wee mouth open wide
In wonder and amazement at everything I spied.

I'd feed my pennies in the slots, and I would stand and stare
At the Laughing Man, the Gypsy, the old Electric Chair;
I'd even have a gamble, for I would have a go
To try to make my fortune, with three pears in a row. . .

And I'd go and ride the bumpers, while the sparks flew
   overhead,
But all the time I watched the clock with ever-mounting
   dread,
And my poor wee heart was heavy, and filled with
   desolation
When I had to dash from Barry's up to Bangor railway
   station.

If it happened that I'd tuppence left (and if the train was
   late),
I'd go and punch my name out on an aluminium plate;
I'd make the odd mistake or two, and the end result looked
   queer,
But at least I'd gone and got myself a Bangor souvenir!

Well, that was many years ago, my childhood's long since
   gone,
And now my hair is turning grey, and I am getting on,
But still I've got a yearning to go there once again,
So excuse me, now – I'm heading off . . . to catch the Bangor
   train!

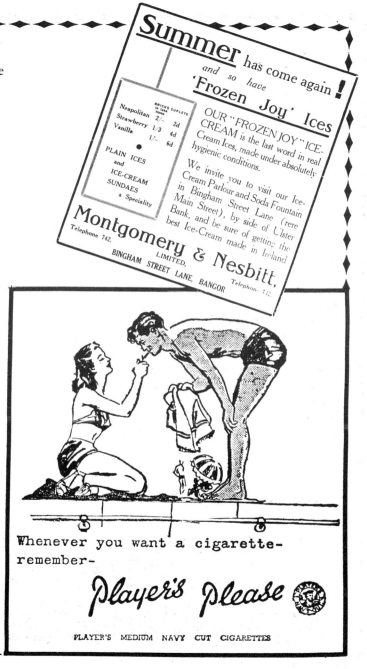

John Castles

If travel broadens the mind, then John Castles must be the most broad-minded guest to take part in 'Day by Day'. John's business is travel which means that on many occasions during the year he goes off on his travels to places far and near, and all in the interests of the rest of us. Keeping in touch with the latest developments on the holiday front is obviously important in a world where circumstances change with greater frequency with each passing year. But John's first taste of travel at the tender age of nine took place much nearer home. Which is why our local resorts mean so much to him.

Are there any Sharks here?

Often, since childhood, I've thought that holidays were changing. On reflection I realise I was never thinking too deeply about it, and in fact when you do stop to consider, there really have been tremendous changes in holiday patterns in our Province, from the time when only the rich could afford a stay at the seaside to a situation where the modern-day 'wealthy' seldom frequent Bangor, Warrenpoint, Newcastle or Portrush.

Whether or not you wish it, there emerges a class consciousness over the years. Debatably the upper classes have not lost any of their prestige, but those who looked on in days gone by, are now part of the scene.

Some of the changes have perhaps had a traumatic effect on some of the participants. Such as Joe Kranstofel, an Austrian violin-player who for a living served afternoon tea in the Northern Counties Hotel in Portrush, long before it came into the hands of the Fawcett family, and not so long after the days when Lord Northcliffe of the *Daily Mail* used to arrive with his retinue, and not one, but two Rolls-Royces.

Accustomed as he was to serving the upper crust, Joe one day noticed a lady with three children come into the lounge of the hotel. She didn't look the part of the elegant ladies Joe normally attended, but as though oblivious to her obvious lack of class, Joe took her order, and duly set up the tea and scones for mother and her three young chicks.

Silver service teapot and jugs may have been appreciated. So too the saucers in their delicate china. Mum poured the tea into cups, and thence, as was obviously her wont, into the saucers for the cooling thus obtained at home. And though to her the charge for such elegant service was perhaps almost frightening, she did pay up, and left, having experienced something different to what everyday life would have offered her outside those elegant doors at a fraction of the price.

In later years, a blow-out for the working classes would, of course, become a fortnight in Majorca or some such exotic area which in a short time would become less exotic and more of an accepted part of life.

But back to those earlier days – to yesterday in holiday terms, and to the grandeur of another famous old hotel, the Slieve Donard at Newcastle, where I've often enjoyed lunch with my family, but where at one time I could not have gone. Economics would have been my main barrier, had I been here at the time when my late father had five shillings a week for working in a linen factory from six in the morning till six at night. At the same time, I can remember being told by Jimmy Faulkner, a former head porter at the Slieve Donard that there were days when the locals wouldn't have got through the front door, at least not to fraternise with the customers. And my same informant told me that when he started he needed references from a doctor, a minister, a priest *and* a schoolteacher, so difficult was it to reach the standards required in those days.

FAWCETT'S TOURS & HOTELS

FAWCETT'S ANTRIM ARMS HOTEL, ANTRIM
HEADQUARTERS OF FAWCETT'S HOLIDAY TOURS, PARTY OF
TOURISTS LEAVING HOTEL FOR DAILY TOUR

Dancing ♣ ♣ ♣ Concerts

SPECIAL FEATURES.

You are assured of a good holiday if you book on **FAWCETT'S TOURS**. We understand your requirements and have the facilities for gratifying them. We have our own large well-equipped Hotels and control our Motor Cars and Coaches, so that our Tours and Hotels are under our own management, which enables us to give the very best service at a reasonable price. Our coaches are up-to-date, sun saloon, safety, with reliable drivers.

Our permanent, competent, native Guide-Lecturers in uniform accompany visitors throughout the Tours, and halt at every place of interest and explain fully, as none others can, the legends and history attached thereto. Hosts and hostesses are always available in the Hotels, and personally look after your comfort and enjoyment.

Our Hotels contain most up-to-date ballrooms with maple floors, modern ventilation and high ceilings. Resident orchestras.

Our Dining-rooms are most comfortable, luxuriously furnished and carpeted. Small tables and complete service to each, so that you can arrange your family parties. All cutlery and plate is Sheffield's best.

Our Hotels are centrally heated. Hot and Cold water all bedrooms.

Ample and comfortable lounges, also commodious new separate ladies' and gents' cloakroom accommodation.

We are members of Ulster Tourist Association, A.A., R.A.C., and R.I A.C.

ELECTRIC PASSENGER LIFT TO ALL FLOORS IN OUR ROYAL PORTRUSH HOTEL

Fawcett's are the only Tours which include the Capital of Northern Ireland and the Capital of the Irish Free State in their itinerary without extra charge, also a visit to Derry City.

We specialise in our tourist business, which receives our best service, accommodation, and personal attention. We guarantee satisfaction.

PLEASE NOTE.—FAWCETT'S are the only Tours where four meals per day are provided without extra charge.

VARIED ENTERTAINMENT PROVIDED IN HOTEL EACH EVENING WITHOUT EXTRA CHARGE

Avoid disappointment by booking early and having your accommodation guaranteed, as we had to refuse hundreds during past seasons.

WEEKLY AND FORTNIGHTLY PROGRAMME

INCLUSIVE PRICES :

"A" TOUR	"B" TOUR
Headquarters: ROYAL PORTRUSH HOTEL PORTRUSH	Headquarters: DUNLAMBERT HOTEL BELFAST
£5 : 12 : 6	**£5 : 12 : 6**

From arrival in Ulster until departure

14 DAY TOURS AND HOTELS
"A" & "B" Tours Itinerary Combined

7 days "A" Tour with Headquarters at Royal Portrush Hotel and 7 days "B" Tour with Headquarters at Dunlambert Hotel, Fortwilliam Park, giving complete change of scenery every day

£11 : 5 : 0

From arrival in Ulster until departure

Daily Menus

ON SATURDAYS

BREAKFAST—Grape Fruit, Bacon and Eggs, Bread (various), Butter, Marmalade, Tea, Coffee.
DINNER—Kidney Soup, Roast Beef, Sauces, Vegetables, Mashed Potatoes, Apple Tart, Cheese and Biscuits, Tea or Coffee.
HIGH TEA—Cold Tongue, Vegetable Salad, Tea, Bread (various), Butter, Preserves. Cake or Scones.
SUPPER—Tea or Coffee and Biscuits.

ON SUNDAYS

BREAKFAST—Grape Fruit, Force, Grape-Nuts, Corn Flakes, Rice Flakes, Stewed Prunes, Porridge, Bacon and Eggs, Tomatoes, Bread (various), Butter, Marmalade, Tea, Coffee.
DINNER—Vegetable Soup, Roast Lamb, Mint Sauce, Peas, Mashed Potatoes, Peach Melba, Cheese, Biscuits, Tea, Coffee.
HIGH TEA—Chicken and Ham, Salad, Tea, Bread (various), Butter, Preserves. Cake or Scones.
SUPPER—Tea or Coffee and Biscuits.

ON MONDAYS

BREAKFAST—Grape Fruit, Force, Grape Nuts, Corn Flakes, Rice Flakes, Stewed Prunes, Porridge, Bacon and Eggs or Cold Ham, Bread (various), Butter, Marmalade, Tea, Coffee.
DINNER—Tomato Soup, Roast Beef, Yorkshire Pudding, Sauces, Vegetables, Boiled Potatoes, Custard and Jelly, Cheese, Biscuits, Tea, Coffee.
HIGH TEA—Salmon Mayonnaise, Tea, Bread (various), Butter, Preserves, Cake or Scones.
SUPPER—Tea or Coffee and Biscuits.

ON TUESDAYS

BREAKFAST—Grape Fruit, Force, Grape-Nuts, Corn Flakes, Rice Flakes, Stewed Prunes, Porridge, Bacon and Eggs, Sausages, Bread (various), Butter, Marmalade, Tea, Coffee.
DINNER—Ox-Tail Soup, Chicken and Ham, Sauces, Vegetables, Mashed Potatoes, Baked Jam Roll, Cheese, Biscuits, Tea, Coffee.
HIGH TEA—Fish, Tea, Bread (various), Butter, Preserves, Cake or Scones.
SUPPER—Tea or Coffee and Biscuits.

ON WEDNESDAYS

BREAKFAST—Grape Fruit, Force, Grape-Nuts, Corn Flakes, Rice Flakes, Stewed Prunes, Porridge, Bacon and Eggs, Tomatoes, Bread (various), Butter, Marmalade, Tea, Coffee.
DINNER—Cream Soup, Roast Lamb, Sauce, Vegetables, Boiled Potatoes, Fruit Salad, Cheese, Biscuits, Tea, Coffee.
HIGH TEA—Cold Ham, Vegetable Salad, Tea, Bread (various), Butter, Preserves, Cake or Scones.
SUPPER—Tea or Coffee and Biscuits.

ON THURSDAYS

BREAKFAST—Grape Fruit, Force, Grape-Nuts, Corn Flakes, Rice Flakes, Stewed Prunes, Porridge, Bacon and Eggs, Bread (various), Butter, Marmalade, Tea, Coffee.
DINNER—Mutton Broth, Roast Pork and Apple Sauce, Vegetables, Mashed Potatoes, Trifle, Cheese, Biscuits, Tea, Coffee.
HIGH TEA—Chicken and Ham, Tea, Bread (various), Butter, Preserves, Cake or Scones.
SUPPER—Tea or Coffee and Biscuits.

ON FRIDAYS

BREAKFAST—Grape Fruit, Force, Grape-Nuts, Corn Flakes, Rice Flakes, Stewed Prunes, Porridge, Bacon and Eggs or Fish, Bread (various), Butter, Marmalade, Tea, Coffee.
DINNER—Lentil Soup, Fried Fillet Haddock, Parsley Sauce, Roast Joint, Sauces, Vegetables, Boiled Potatoes, Peach Melba, Cheese, Biscuits, Tea, Coffee.
HIGH TEA—Lough Neagh Salmon, Mayonnaise, Tea, Bread (various), Butter, Preserves, Cake or Scones.
SUPPER—Tea or Coffee and Biscuits.

FISH can be had as an alternative breakfast menu, if a note to that effect is given to your waiter at the previous breakfast table.
FRUIT SALAD can be had in lieu of any tea menu during the week, notice being given not later than the previous meal.
The above menus are guaranteed for Season 1939 by FAWCETT'S TOURS AND HOTELS

TIMES OF MEALS.

BREAKFAST daily 9 a.m.		HIGH TEA	6 p.m.
DINNER	1 p.m.	SUPPER	10 p.m.

Our Hotels are supplied Fresh Daily from our Estate at " The Steeple " Hall with Chickens, Eggs, and all Farm Produce, also Vegetables, Fruit, and Flowers.

❶ Fawcett's are the only Tours giving 4 Meals per day without extra charge. *See Menus when comparing Prices and Programmes*

Fawcett's Touring Coaches.

Itinerary "A" Tour

HEADQUARTERS:
ROYAL PORTRUSH HOTEL, PORTRUSH

Over 500 Miles Motoring in Ulster

Arrivals from Scotland, England and Wales

On Saturday mornings and Saturday evenings and Sunday mornings our motor coaches and Guides meet visitors on arrival of boats and trains at Belfast or Larne and convey them with their luggage direct to our Hotels without extra charge. Visitors desiring to join our Tours at any other time will be met by arrangement, or which a reasonable charge will be made.
A substantial meal is served immediately on arrival in the Hotel. Evening Dancing in the Hotel Ballroom.

SUNDAY:
Arrangements are made enabling those wishing to attend Divine Service to do so. Optional bathing and golfing parties arranged. Then, after Dinner, motor drive to the Giant's Causeway, where we pay for your admission into the Causeway proper. Our Guide-Lecturers take you round every point of this wonderful work of nature and explain its mysteries one by one, and tell of its legends. Ample time is given for its thorough exploration, and those with cameras can obtain very interesting snaps. Return via Dunluce Castle, where a halt is made and the origin of the Red Hand of Ulster explained. Back to Hotel for High Tea after a very instructive and enjoyable visit to the Causeway. Evening Concert in Hotel.

MONDAY:
After breakfast leave for 150 miles circular Tour to the City of Belfast, Capital of Northern Ireland. Through Ballymoney to Ballymena, via Harryville and Tallykeel, crossing the River Kellswater at Tannybrock along the picturesque slopes of the Tardree Mountains, you pass through the quaint little village of Doagh, convenient to which is the Hole Stone through which Pagan marriages were performed. Then through Mossley and Cloughfern, along the shores of Belfast Lough to Fortwilliam Park, where mid-day Dinner will be served at our Dunlambert Hotel. In the Hotel Grounds is situated the Fort where King William the Third encamped on his way to the Battle of the Boyne in 1690. After Dinner, games and sports can be indulged in in the Hotel Grounds. Continue the drive to Belfast City, visiting the City Hall, the finest in the British Isles. Ample time is given to visit the principal shopping centres where the shops are open all day. The Tour continues through Antrim where can be seen the original of the Irish Cabin written of in "My Lady of the Chimney Corner." Then through beautiful Irish Demesnes, passing Lough Neagh, and along the Valley of the Bann, arriving in our Portrush Hotel in time for High Tea. Evening : Dancing in the Ballroom of the Hotel.

TUESDAY:
Bathing parade and sports in the forenoon. After early Dinner, interesting Tour to the historic City of Derry, passing through the Valley of the Roe and viewing its lovely Glens : over the Derry Mountains, from which you have an unrivalled view of Lough Foyle and the Hills of Donegal. Our Guide will explain why Derry is called " The Maiden City " and the " Queen of Erin's Daughters " when conducting the party round the city's walls, the building of which took eighteen years. In the Cathedral ancient records and relics may be examined, after which visitors are at leisure to further explore this wonderful old city. Whist Drive in the Hotel in the evening.

WEDNESDAY:
You spend the day in Portrush, the most charming and natural seaside resort in the British Isles. Its innumerable bays are practically as nature left them—here you have a rocky shore and there a beach of golden sands. A short distance out from the shore facing the Hotel, are the Skerry Islands. The clear water in the bays is continually changing colour and the natural promenade of Ramore Head stretches out into the Atlantic. The invigorating air is peculiar to Portrush. No other seaside resort has water or air like Portrush, due to its position on the western coast and uninterrupted Atlantic breezes.
Dancing and Games in Hotel in the evening.

THURSDAY:
After breakfast, sports, bathing and recreation programme arranged. Then leave for ninety miles circular Tour, to visit the beautiful Glens in the Vale of Glenariff, where we pay for your admission to the Glens proper. Our Guide-Lecturers take you round those gorgeous natural and wooded Glens with their delightful walks and exquisite waterfalls, where a pleasant time can be spent. Then a drive along the North Atlantic coast over the famous Coast Road with its ever-changing scenery, where we get a glorious view of Rathlin Island and the Scottish Coast. Carnival Dance in Hotel for which valuable prizes are given.

FRIDAY:
After breakfast, a motor coach drive along the beautiful west Coast Road from which you obtain a wonderful view of the Atlantic Ocean, Lough Foyle, and the Hills of Donegal, visiting the seaside resort of Portstewart. Ample time is given to thoroughly explore this nice little town. Return to Hotel for mid-day dinner. The afternoon is free for packing, exchanging photographs and addresses with newly formed friends, and having a pleasant social evening in Hotel. Those leaving for home on Friday evening via Larne-Stranraer leave the Hotel at 4.30 p.m., then motor through ever-changing scenery to embark on outgoing boat. Those leaving home on Friday night via Belfast boats leave the Hotel at 6 p.m., then a glorious motor drive through beautiful rural scenery (with their luggage) in time to embark on outgoing boat for home.
Arrangements will be made for those proceeding to our "B" Tour Headquarters for the following week.

SATURDAY:
Those leaving for home by daylight boat leave Hotel after breakfast, and have lovely drive to Belfast or Larne, where they join outgoing boat.

VARIED ENTERTAINMENTS PROVIDED IN HOTEL EACH EVENING WITHOUT EXTRA CHARGE

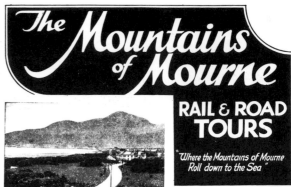

Yet, while there was a great class gap between servant and served, among the latter there were, I'm told, some lovely people who came to the Slieve and similar establishments.

Such as Mr Baines, the baker, who with his family was a regular visitor to Newcastle. A kindly man, recalls Jimmy (who in 1930 earned twenty-five shillings a week, 'less two shillings for a stamp'). Not high wages, but supplemented by tips which made the job most attractive. To the degree that Jimmy can remember one occasion travelling with his bike from Castlewellan to the hotel in snow, which necessitated carrying the bike the last mile or so above his head. But then Christmas was a busy time when all hands were needed in the hotel. After all it needed a horse and cart to carry guests' baggage in a type of shuttle service from the nearby railway station which in those days was served by both the Great Northern and Belfast and County Down systems.

But back to Mr Baines the baker, and a lovely little story about his involvement one morning after breakfast with waiter Joe Halliday, who at the time would also have been earning around twenty five shillings a week. It must have been the day for departure, but Mr Baines handed Joe a five-pound note – one of the big white ones that used to make us feel wealthy when inflation was something to do with the wheels of pushbikes. Carrying a pile of plates, Joe crumpled it up and stuffed it, with thanks to the donor, into his trouser pocket. At which Mr Baines, to Joe Halliday's surprise, asked, 'Is that the way you look after your money?' Joe was asked to return it to the giver, and arrived back in the kitchens nearly in tears. A tip of four weeks' wages in your pocket and gone again?

There was a lot of talk among the staff that morning. But, as they say, all is well that ends well, because Joe Halliday was to have another surprise when the Baines family arrived at table for lunch. After eating, to Joe's surprise and delight, Mr Baines took a nice leather wallet from his pocket, with a crisp new fiver in it, handed both to him and said, 'That is how to keep your money, Joe.'

Those days, and subsequent ones, were to cover a period when Sir Frederick and Lady Rebbeck of the shipyard would be regulars, as would Sir Clarence Graham of Dromore, and the Barbours of Lisburn. Those were the days of salt-water baths in the hotel, supplied by a pipe which still projects, unused, from the Slieve Donard into the sea.

If those were the days of Rolls-Royces and Bentleys for some, they were also to become, between the great wars, the days of the charabanc and subsequently the more salubrious bus, which despite almost non-existent springing, provided a thrilling means of transport for the 'ordinary five-eights' as I can so often remember the working classes referred to.

It cost half a crown to travel on Mickey Sawey's charabanc in Newcastle in those days. While factory workers could afford to pay that sort of money, not many of the girls could have paid the fifteen shillings it cost for a hairdo. It was probably some of the Scottish visitors who said that if a perm was fifteen bob, Mickey Sawey could blow it out again for a sixth of that amount!

Those same Scots were more than likely from the emerging middle classes or they could not have afforded an even greater fare, that of the boat from Glasgow to Belfast.

Entrepreneur that he was, Mickey provided that first charabanc service where the Mountains of Mourne sweep down to the sea. It wasn't just Sir Freddie Laker who in later years was to invent competition. Oh no, because even back in the Thirties it was to be found in Newcastle.

The success and popularity of Mickey Sawey's charabanc service didn't go unnoticed by one Mr Pithers who used to run the Slieve Donard Garage, and provide cover for the Rolls and Bentleys of those who didn't need charabancs. He saw an opportunity of serving a wider section of the public than those who could afford their own transport. And one day, to the annoyance of Mickey

Sawey, he arrived in town with the first closed bus, which, if it offered no other advantage, meant that ladies could keep their hairdos intact.

Off went Mickey to Lancashire to buy a closed bus of his own, and then the fun really started, and folk began to shop around for cheaper travel, as their children and grandchildren would one day do.

And if they didn't come to the bus, the bus effectively came to them. One advert shows that in 1938, you could have an all-day trip from Newcastle to Dublin for ten shillings. However, the late Mickey Sawey's daughter, still living in the town, told me that Charlie Rodgers, a driver, who rode his push-bike to work from the townland of Ballagh, called at hotels and guesthouses on the way to work canvassing for passengers, and indeed if you could muster a party of five or more, the fare dropped to six and sixpence each.

Born and raised in Lurgan, I was perhaps fortunate that we were well-placed for holidays in County Down's three main resorts of Newcastle, Bangor and Warrenpoint, around which we alternated in my childhood days, with the odd trip further afield to Portrush, though for a number of glorious years from 1946 to 1952, I was to 'half-live' in 'The Port', as we called it. An aunt had moved to Coleraine, and I could hardly wait for the end of each June, when I would ritually cry as my mother put me on the train at Lurgan station for Belfast, where my Aunt Cissie would come down from Oldpark to transport me safely to York Road, and put me on another train for Coleraine. Travel must always have been in my blood, because I started travelling around Ireland at nine years of age.

Those were the days of cheap season tickets which permitted unlimited journeys between any two points. Such as Coleraine and Portrush. In those days, with new-found pals Willie Edgar, Don Galbraith, Henry Gregg (later known as Harry, with Manchester United and Ireland), I really made use of those tickets. We had little pocket money in those days, but that didn't matter.

What we had we valued, and used to best advantage — little criminals that we sometimes were. The train from Portrush would arrive in Coleraine station through the level crossing. I remember some of the boys setting a ha'penny on the line before the train arrived, so that when it went into the station it made the coin look more like a penny, which would sometimes work the slot machines in Barry's when we got there.

Many's a day a flat ha'penny provided a number of boys from the Bushmills Road with a toffee apple or ice cream. That was all we spent our money on. Toilets would have been a lavish means of spending one's hard-earned cash, when one could use the season ticket back to Coleraine, get to the toilet at home and come back on the same train before it returned to 'the Port'.

How expert too some of those boys were in memorising the sequence of the slot machines. I still remember that if red came up on the Wheel of Fortune, the prize was twopence; the same with green; though the ultimate was (I believe) white, which rattled out twenty pennies — a real fortune.

Criminals in a sense, but really no badness in us. We would never have dreamed of chasing each other around Portrush with hatchets, as some of our counterparts would do in years to come.

Our biggest thrills, and on a personal basis, *my* biggest thrills, came from helping with the donkeys on the strand at Portrush, or pushing out and pulling in rowing boats, be they in the pond at Newcastle, or the harbour at Portrush; not forgetting the fleet at Bangor. At one time this totalled over one hundred skiffs and punts operating in high season for ten and twelve hours a day. Over the years, this has diminished to a fraction of that, finding four busy hours a day a lucrative operation, though prices generally haven't risen with the cost of living.

 THE TRIP TO PORTRUSH

The weather was killin'
    This last wheen o' weeks,
And the ladies were losin'
    The bloom off their cheeks ;
But they're going to get back
    What they lost of their blush,
When we go, on the fifth,
    To the sea at Portrush.

John Willie has bought
    A new dickie and tie,
And is usin' cold tay
    On his hair for a dye,
In a pair of "plus fours"
    And a waistcoat of plush,
He'll cut a quare dash
    On the fifth at Portrush.

My missus has purchased
    A canty wee hat,
And a short parasol—
    From Woolworth's—mind that !
Who cares if we get
    A wee squeeze or a push
When we're out for the day
    On a trip to Portrush.

The girls from Newtown',
    The Bridge and the Plum,
And bingle-haired beauties
    From Omey will come,
And the chap who won't coort,
    We will label "Don't crush !"
In a car by himself
    On the trip to Portrush.

As for my own self,
    I'll say nothing at all,
But I want to get next
    To some good-looking doll,
In a dolly-dyed jumper
    That stands a good crush,
I might give her a glam
    On the road to Portrush.

So now I have come
    To the end of my rhyme,
Mulcaghey must hustle
    And work overtime ;
If I have to eat nettles
    Or diet on mush
I'll be there on the fifth.
    When we go to Portrush

A Night in an Ulster Youth Hostel

It was about half-past-five in the evening when I saw the familiar Youth Hostel sign and, turning down a narrow side road, a couple of minutes' walk brought me to the hostel.

A low, white-washed cottage—as I entered I found myself in a kitchen living-room of a moderate size, in which there were eight or nine young people of both sexes. Two girls were clearing away the remains of their meal, while at the other end of the table two other girls were busily engaged in laying out crockery and cutlery for their party, which had evidently just arrived. Several other people sat round the big fireplace. One young man was putting a film in his camera, another was darning his sock, a girl was reading a two months old copy of "Woman and Home", while her companion gazed reflectively into the fire, engaged in day dreams.

Through a door in the opposite wall I could see into a small annexe, which was evidently used for cooking, and from which came the friendly roar of several Primus stoves going at once and the appetising smell of frying bacon, together with the sound of several very Scottish voices raised in song.

As I entered, everyone looked up and gave me a friendly "Good evening", and I asked the invariable question: "Where's the men's dormitory and the warden's house, please?" The men's dormitory was separate from the hostel proper and had at one time evidently been an outhouse of some sort. (The women's dormitory was in the hostel and opened off the living-room.) It was a bare room of moderate size with a stone floor and lighted by one small window. It contained four of the usual "double-deckers" which take the place of beds in Youth Hostels. A "double-decker" consists of a stout wooden frame about four-and-a-half feet high, which holds two canvas bunks, one above the other. The only other furniture in the room was a wooden box upon which was set an enamel basin for washing, a small and much stained mirror, and two oil lamps. Each person staying at the hostel is required to provide his own sheet-bag, but is supplied with four blankets, and, following the principle of "one under and three over", I soon had my bed made up.

Having signed the book in the warden's house, I returned to the hostel and prepared my tea. It was eight o'clock by the time that the last party arrived, had their tea and washed up, and joined the circle of some dozen or fourteen people which was formed round the blazing fire.

Conversation ran on a variety of subjects, and, from my previous experience of Ulster hostels in the holiday season, I was not at all surprised to find that I was the only Ulsterman present—all the others being from Scotland, England or Southern Ireland. We sang for some time, the songs ranging from "The Garden where the Praties Grow" to "Bonnie Charlie's Gone Awa'", and then, when the singing slackened, I suddenly said: "Would anyone like to learn an Irish dance?" Everyone said "Yes" at once, so I fetched my mouthorgan and, after a little instruction, four of the English and Scots members were busily, and not unskilfully, engaged in dancing the "Siege of Carric", while I reflected on the strangeness of the fact that English people in particular always seem to take to Irish dancing even more keenly than Irish people do themselves. A Scots girl then tried to teach us a Sword Dance, and, after doing another Irish dance, we wound up with the "Palais Glide", and went to bed.

Next morning, having washed and shaved in cold water with the aid of the aforementioned enamel basin and stained mirror, I dressed and went into the living-room, where there was great activity. One party was cooking breakfast, a second party eating, and a third washing up. After breakfast there was the usual scurry to get the hostel tidied and the blankets shaken before departure. As usual, this was done with much willingness and enthusiasm, but with complete lack of organisation, with the result that while the living-room was swept three times nobody cleaned the Primus stove bench.

When I felt that I had done my share, I said "Good-bye" all round, exchanged one or two addresses, hitched my rucksack on to my shoulders, and started down the road.

For the moment I felt sorry. My brief stay at the hostel had been a happy one, the crowd a jolly one, and I should probably never meet any of them again. However, it was a sunny morning and in the evening I should reach another hostel with another happy band in it. I hitched my rucksack a little higher on my shoulders and stepped out briskly.

Boyd Harris.

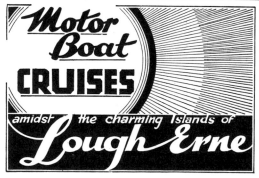

It is a boating memory that is outstanding in my recollections of Warrenpoint, though this particular experience bears out the story of the visitor once asking before going for a swim, 'Are there any sharks here?' to be told he was safe in the water as all the sharks were on dry land.

What an exciting morning it was for me. A lot of 'rhyming on' from me brought from Dad an agreement that we should invest in an hour's rowing session down beside the swimming pool. Being first there, we were told quite clearly that although the two shillings covered an hour, we need not be too particular about being on time when we returned. I wanted to row around the rock that can be seen from the promenade at Warrenpoint (or at least it could be in those days), and we were ten minutes over our time.

I thought my father was going to fight with the boatman when he demanded another shilling for an extra half hour or part of it, as we had stayed over an hour. He didn't get the shilling, I can tell you.

Perhaps Warrenpoint is the most changed of our resorts, because whereas Bangor and Portrush retained their railway, and Newcastle retained its popularity, thus encouraging travel by bus when the railways closed, Warrenpoint (and locals agree with me on this) was only to suffer its final blow when the trains stopped. It could probably be described as a victim of circumstances not of its own making. However one might have spent the rest of the week in Warrenpoint, for most, Sunday evening would be spent sitting on the wall watching the boats arrive from Omeath.

Sabbath drinking being taboo in the North, full trains used to arrive from Belfast on Sundays, but not for a day in Warrenpoint. Instead the attraction was the Red Star Line motor-boat service across the Lough (or in one of the rival boats). Then in the evening the drinkers would return providing such macabre sights as fur-coated women in drunken stupor, falling into the tide instead of coming down the sloping plank that provided contact

Holiday Reminders

YOU'LL TAKE all the family's ration books—of course ! Hotels and boarding-houses require them if you stay for five nights or longer. If you have deposited any pages of coupons with your shopkeeper, get these back and take them with you.

If you are going to do your own housekeeping, or stay with friends, you'll need a temporary ration card covering the number of weeks you'll be away. It's easier and quicker to get this at your local Food Office before you go. *Please try to do this.*

It's advisable to buy your sweet ration before you go and take it with you.

Don't forget to take soap with you, too.

Before you go away be sure to cancel standing orders for milk, bread, and any other foods.

IDEAS FOR PICNIC MEALS

HIGHLAND PIE

8 oz. raw minced meat; 3 oz. minced or finely chopped onion; 2 level teaspoons flour; 2-3 level teaspoons salt; ¼ level teaspoon pepper; 2 teaspoons of a Worcester sauce; 6-8 tablespoons water; 6 oz. short-crust pastry.

Mix the meat, onion, flour and seasoning together and add the sauce and water. Line a 7-in. sandwich tin with half the pastry, add the meat mixture and cover with the remaining pastry. Make a 1-in. slit in the pastry cover and bake in a hot oven for 25-30 minutes; reduce the heat to moderate and cook for a further 15-25 minutes.

CHEESE-AND ONION TURNOVERS

6 oz. pastry; 2-3 oz. grated cheese; 4 level tablespoons breadcrumbs; 1 onion, chopped finely; a little milk or stock; salt and pepper.

Roll out the pastry and cut into 4-in. squares. Mix together the cheese, breadcrumbs and onion. Add enough milk or stock to make a soft consistency. Season well. Put a little of the mixture into the centre of each square of pastry, moisten the edges and fold over the pastry cornerwise to form triangles. Press the edges firmly down, brush with a little reconstituted egg, and bake in a moderate oven till brown.

SANDWICH-FILLING IDEAS

SAVOURY : *Grated cheese, made to a paste with a little milk and seasoning. Corned beef flaked and mixed with a little sweet chutney. A lettuce leaf improves almost all sandwich fillings.*

SWEET : *Chopped dates; lemon curd; grated chocolate; jam or marmalade.*

Use bread that is a day old, and cut in ¼ to ⅛-in. slices. Spread one slice thinly with margarine and spread the other slice with the filling.

Pack sandwiches in greaseproof paper. In very hot weather, if the sandwiches are prepared some time in advance, it's best to wrap them in an old table-napkin wrung out of cold water as soon as they're made. A large lettuce leaf also makes a cool, fresh wrapping.

★ ★ ★

If you're taking tea in a vacuum flask, take the *milk* separately. You'll find the tea tastes much better this way.

THIS IS WEEK **2**—THE SECOND WEEK OF RATION PERIOD No. 1 (July 20th to August 16th)

ISSUED BY THE MINISTRY OF FOOD, LONDON, S.W.1. FOOD FACTS No. 38

between the ship and land. Despite my youth, I can well remember being glad I didn't come from a drinking family, because had that been the case I would have had to stand before 'Him' for interrogation. I never knew 'his' name, but he was the toughest of the customs men at Warrenpoint, and the gallery along the wall used to just say, 'Here's Him', and you knew who they meant. He seemed to bring more into the search hut than anyone else, and when they had been in with him, they seemed to come out with fewer parcels than they had carried from the boat. However, while mass travel was to bring prosperity to transit ports like Dover and Calais, it was effectively to kill a part of Warrenpoint's tourism, because the point was reached where 'decent' people wouldn't get on the same train to Belfast as the drunks, and other resorts were to benefit accordingly.

Self-catering was popular in those days and especially in Warrenpoint where families from Lurgan, Portadown, and further afield would 'take' a house for a month, and probably pay only £10 or £20 for the privilege. Few would have dreamed in those days of families paying a hundred times more for self-catering in Barbados – which today would be in the financial range of the same professional people.

Looking back can bring many nostalgic memories, but doesn't there have to be a degree of sadness to see the departure of that wonderful tram from Portrush to Bushmills and the Giant's Causeway, or the noisy throbbing of Barry's Amusements in what was the Grand Hotel overlooking Bangor harbour? Conversely, some would 'mourn' the introduction of the throbbing music of the Disco to Bangor's Royal Hotel where space was once allotted, as a public service, at the back of the old hotel for a town morgue.

Some I spoke to recently referred to the past as the 'good old days', when people like Eddie Laird could rent out their boats without the renters apparently thinking the rental fee gave them the right to wreck them as though they had bought them and they were their own. Others

like one landlady at Ballyholme feel that we are only now in the 'good old days' where money is more evenly spread around, and there is more of it for more people to enjoy a holiday at the seaside. Others in local tourism feel that seaside holidays are being spent to a greater degree in foreign lands, while the local resorts are used more for day trips by car, train or bus.

If that be true, and I suppose looking at it realistically there is more than a modicum of truth in it, then perhaps the Loves and the Castles of later generations might hold their heads in shame for the part they have played in encouraging the natives to leave these lovely shores of ours, extolling, Day by Day, the virtues of lands which yesterday our forefathers could hardly have dreamt of seeing.

ON THE PROMENADE, WHITEHEAD

Patricia Mencarelli

One of Northern Ireland's top models, Patricia made her initial impact on the fashion world while still in her teens. She was featured on the front covers of 'Vogue', 'Woman' and 'Woman's Own', as well as making her appearance in leading London fashion shows. Patricia's early interest in fashion was encouraged by her mother and by her Aunt Olga, and she still rememembers some important early advice – 'Buy little, buy good.' With her colleague Grace Emanuel, Patricia started her own School of Modelling. Our leading Commere, Patricia is less well known as a teacher of Ballet and Yoga.

Flights of Fashion

Fashion has a habit of repeating itself. Styles, once popular in a past decade, can reappear to captivate the fashion-conscious of another age, and this is just as true in Northern Ireland as anywhere else. So let us fly away on a fanciful flight round the world of fabulous fashion.

Our take-off point is the Roaring Twenties and our landing will see us into the Adventurous Fifties. So it's back to round about the year 1920 in our imaginary parade of fashion to where the boyish figures of my models are topped by short bobbed shingled hairstyles. The line just now is cylinder shape, and belts are anywhere but on the waist line.

THE SWING OF THE PENDULUM.

IT IS PERHAPS JUST AS WELL—

THAT THE TWENTIETH-CENTURY GIRL—

AFTER HAVING BOBBED HER HAIR—

THEN SHINGLED IT—

THEN ADOPTED THE ETON CROP—

NEVER QUITE REACHED THE DARTMOOR SHAVE—

AND IS NOW STARTING TO GROW IT (AND HER DRESS) AGAIN.

Greta loves her straight chemise in georgette. It's a heavenly shade of blue, huge belt surrounding the hips, and loads of tiny beads falling to just below the waist, as she mimics the Charleston down the ramp.

Lizzie is casual – it's called the pyjama look – with wide-bottomed wool slacks, striped cotton sleeveless T shirt for less formal wear.

Nanette has chosen a cocktail dress, encrusted with tiny sequins. Deep scoop neckline, and look at that crazy hem, up at the front and down at the back. I love her cloche hat and her Mona Lisa smile peering from under it, not a trace of hair in sight.

As usual, Grace is late, roaring up in her reckless open-topped automobile, long scarf flowing behind her. She's wearing a super navy wool suit with a long fingertip-length jacket, white piqué lapels and the fashionable chemise underneath, and, to complete the effect, tiny-heeled red shoes and a matching bag.

And now the orchestra comes to a crescendo, the wedding guests are here, pink and grey is the theme for the finale. The bride looks stunning in pure silk. Her wedding dress is softest grey and she has the loveliest pull-on cloche hat, sisal straw trimmed with lace.

NIGHTWEAR AND DRESSING GOWNS

Special Autumn Sale

CE72. Dressing Gown in warm Ripple Cloth, narrow inset sleeves, revere and cuffs finished narrow bands of satin and fancy stitching; length 50 ins. in rose, crimson, light saxe, amethyst, dark saxe. **14/11**

CE73. Night Gown in cream Nunsveiling, neck and sleeves piped in colours, flowers to tone; v neck **Each 7/6**

CE76. Knickers, directoire shape, in Natural Schappe Silk, embroidered with spray on legs; sky, pink, peach, green. **Per Pair 6/6** In Self Colourings **8/11**

CE74. Night Gown in cream Nunsveiling, neck and sleeves piped in colours flowers to tone; round neck. **Each 7/11**

CE77. Bed Jacket in fine Wool, with long sleeves, pink, white, self colours **Each 6/11**

CE75. Night Gown Natural Schappe Si_ piped in sky, peac_ green, pink, flower embroidered to tone. **Each 12/6**

As above, in self colours. **Each 14/6**

ROBINSON & CLEAVER, LTD., THE ROYAL IRISH LINEN HOUSE, BELFAST

Advice to readers of 'The Ulster Countrywoman' in 1938.

FASHION NOTES

Have you started to think of what you will wear next winter?

The shops have cleared the last remnants of the Sales from their windows, and the new models are appearing. These are simple, but clever. Therein lies the secret of chic for 1939.

If you wish to look really Parisienne, you must be high-hatted this season. Crowns rise high, and are folded in becoming lines. Brims are usually small and curve upwards, but some are large and waving. If you are going to have one of the latter, be sure that your neck and shoulder line has only flat trimmings. Otherwise you will look "fussy" and will spoil the sweeping line of your brim.

If you feel you must wear a small hat, let it have one piece of decoration only—enormous bows on mere skull caps are both becoming and amusing, and fur caps are "in" again.

Suits have gone military with braid and buttons. Shoulders are wide, but not padded. Plain coats are worn with brightly checked skirts. Slightly more "dressy" is the soft, woolly cloth frock, with jacket of the same material, faintly checked, and flat fur revers. Long coats have flat fur collars or borders of dyed fox.

The most fashionable gatherings of the year have proved that for practical purposes the long afternoon frock is definitely out. The new dresses are short, plain in cut, but of lovely, heavy materials.

In evening fabrics, georgette and chiffon seem to have come into their own again. Dresses are of pastel hues, the material gathered in soft ruchings. Styles are convenient in that they are varied, and you may wear what suits you best. The picture frock is still a favourite, but no longer has puffed sleeves. The new version has narrow straps, or is off one shoulder.

It is surprising that more people who spend evenings at home have not taken to wearing house-coats. They are so much more comfortable than any other form of dress, and are very cheap either to buy or to make. They should be ankle length, full-skirted, and made of any gay material you like. Cretonne is as effective as anything.

Lastly, what colours are you going to choose? Decide upon one basic colour with which a variety of shades may be worn. The newest are deep cherry, dark moss green, and gunmetal grey. Black is ever increasing in popularity, so much so that it may become common. Tan seems to have faded into the background.

But, whatever you choose, be sure that your whole outfit, from the top of your high hat to the toes of your shoes, fits in to your colour scheme, and BE SIMPLE.

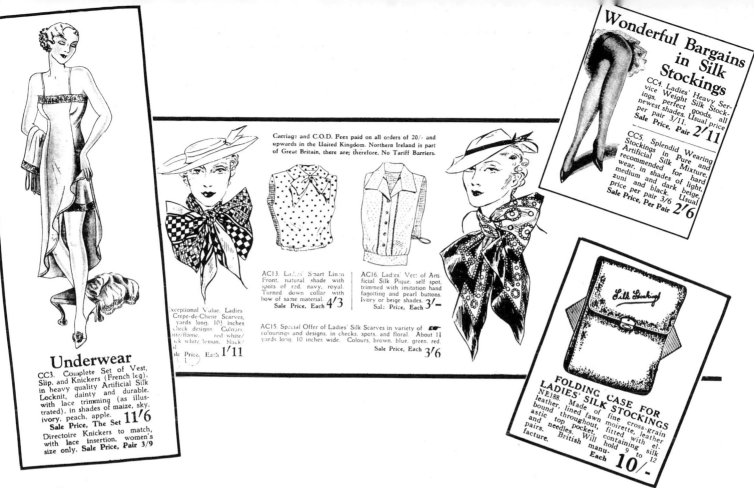

Underwear

CC3. Complete Set of Vest, Slip, and Knickers (French leg), in heavy quality Artificial Silk Locknit, dainty and durable, with lace trimming (as illustrated), in shades of maize, sky, ivory, peach, apple. **Sale Price, The Set 11/6**
Directoire Knickers to match, with lace insertion, women's size only. **Sale Price, Pair 3/9**

Carriage and C.O.D. Fees paid on all orders of 20/- and upwards in the United Kingdom. Northern Ireland is part of Great Britain, there are; therefore, No Tariff Barriers.

Exceptional Value. Ladies' Crepe-de-Chene Scarves, yards long, 10½ inches check designs. Colours white/flame, red white/black white, lemon, black/ Sale Price, Each **1/11**

AC13. Ladies' Smart Linen Front, natural shade with spots of red, navy, royal. Turned down collar with bow of same material. Sale Price, Each **4/3**

AC16. Ladies' Vest of Artificial Silk Pique, self spot, trimmed with imitation hand fagotting and pearl buttons. Ivory or beige shades. Sale Price, Each **3/-**

AC15. Special Offer of Ladies' Silk Scarves in variety of colourings and designs, in checks, spots, and floral. About 1½ yards long, 10 inches wide. Colours, brown, blue, green, red. Sale Price, Each **3/6**

Taxiing into the 1930s, it's a different venue, change of models. Most of the Thirties model girls are married. Here comes Wendy, almost a Mrs Simpson look-alike – simplicity of line, superb cut; a fine cotton dress, with huge puff sleeves – and the waistline is back again!

Tweed suits with military shoulders are in; the skirt length is about 14 ins off the floor – 'Very practical for the country,' Fanny murmurs as she swings down the catwalk, her little trilby hat perched on the front of her head.

I love the Chanel suit Sally wears – so adaptable. Edge to edge jacket and flared skirt, all in honey-brown tweed; a gold satin blouse peeping out underneath, and loads of crystal beads float over the top.

Here comes Sandra looking like Jean Harlow, a slight wriggle as she strolls around the ramp in a film-star gown topped with tiny pearls, shoe-string straps, and really that skirt is very tight, flaring down to the full hemline – altogether a softer, more feminine line. Greta Garbo, Marlene Dietrich, Vivien Leigh, Joan Crawford, these are today's stars and their influence is evident.

The Right Sort of Frocks

Easy-to-make Fashions Designed Specially for Wear in the Home

We can send you perfect patterns of these frocks for 1/- each, in bust sizes 32, 34, 36, 38, and 40. Send your orders to Woman's Own, The Pattern Shop, 12 Southampton Street, Strand, London, W.C.2.

A Message to YOU

THERE are two sorts of women in the world.

Silly girls who spend all the money they can lay their hands on over the draper's counter. Worthy women who say to themselves: "He didn't marry me for my looks," and cheerfully spend every penny they can scrape together on the children—the house —but *never* on themselves.

They are each as wrong as the other. What I want you all to do is to strike the happy middle way between the two.

He may not fathom the difference between silk and cotton, especially if the colour is blue to match your eyes, but he will notice—none quicker— if you cease to be the attractive, alluring girl he married.

Resolve—very early in your married life—never to get slack about your appearance—and when you've made a dainty frock, don't be afraid to wear it. It's sometimes easy to overlook special occasions, you know. When Jim says: "What about the pictures to-night?" don't be tempted to feel that your day frock will do—"it's only Jim." Show your appreciation by slipping into your very nicest dress— "*because* it's Jim.". You used to, when you were engaged, didn't you?

A gay frock isn't a luxury, it's an investment! Try it and see. And if you're in any doubt about the materials or the making, or any other sewing problem, remember that I'm here to help you. I shall love to hear from you.

Your friend,

AMELIA.

No. 29048

A little frock in printed rayon in your wardrobe means that you need never hesitate when a neighbour asks you to slip over that very evening with your husband to meet a few friends. This frock is simplicity itself to cut and to make, yet it has the correct shaped-to-the-figure hip-yoke, full sleeves set into narrow cuff bands, and a frilled cowl collar. The narrow sash matches, of course. In a frock like this you'll feel perfectly at ease when you give those first important tea parties. Allow 4 yds. of 38-in. material for the 36-in. bust size.

No. 29050

No. 29049

(Left). Curved side panels to a skirt are very slimming; they allow a pretty flare about the ankles, too. A frock on these lines (No. 29049) would look its best in a silk or crêpe marocain, or perhaps satin; choose one of the attractive burgundy reds or African brown. If you have Irish crochet by you, now is the time to use it for collar and cuffs; if not, the new starched lace would make a perfect collar and sleeve trimmings. You will need 3¼ yds. of 38-in. material and ⅜ yd. of 36-in. lace for trimming. (Above). Puffed sleeves give a youthful air to an informal frock of old-world patterned silk. The long shoulder line is very new. Allow 3¼ yds. of 38-in. material.

" There are women who can carry off the postilion chapeau with success; of all I like best the Renaissance beret."

FASHIONABLE INFORMATION

NEVER in the history of clothes-conscious women has black been left out of the fashion list for more than a season or so. It is not suprising, therefore, to hear that the Parisienne has gone all out for it again. She appears trimly clad in a neat black linen, silk, or thin wool suit in the morning. Later she is seen in one of the desirable frocks which go variously by the names of "afternoon," "tea-time," and "cinema." They may even be christened "cocktail" if they are sufficiently interesting to appear about six o'clock and carry on amiably through the rest of the evening. At dinner and dance the *chic* lady of Paris parades again her black gown—chiffon, maybe, satin, lace, cloque, or any one of the many new materials with exciting new names which have been introduced by the experts this season.

Skirt length? No change. Morning and afternoon lengths remain as they were. Evening gowns are made with skirts which just touch the floor—trains, by the way, are definitely on the decrease; women found them too tiresome when dancing, and so, wisely, they abandoned them.

The frock which was described as "picture" has not had a very long life. The debutante still likes it, but the older woman has adopted the softly draped style, which, though it calls for the perfect figure, has at least the grace to show off that figure to perfection. Any kind of drapery is fashionable. You can go all Greek and feel quite in the swim, while the Egyptian and the Indian arrangements are suggested by designers for clients whom these draperies suit and who can afford to buy many gowns.

Hand Work.

Pleats are seen everywhere. So are tucks, and some of the most attractive effects on evening as well as day frocks are obtained by means of close shirring, gauging, honey-combing, faggot-stitching, and various other kinds of hand work which take up much of the dressmaker's time and are charged for accordingly. But this does not mean that the pretty individual touches cannot be enjoyed by the woman of more restricted means. Charming little blouses can be made with reliable paper patterns as guides for cutting, and these can be treated by the amateur with the dainty hand work which spells personality. Incidentally, it is still permissible to wear a blouse of chiffon or georgette or lamé in the evening with a graceful skirt, so part of the dinner-dress problem is also solved for the home dressmaker who has ideas.

Speaking of pleats and honey-combing, one of the most successful models shown at a recent collection was developed in black chiffon, the skirt finely pleated from the waist, the bodice cut quite simply, and both waistline and yokeline marked with rows of honey-combing. The model also illustrated the new full sleeves—cut in one with the bodice, fullness at the tops regulated by honey-combing and again at the wrists by similar work. This was a fascinating gown, made more so by the upstanding frill collar of stiffened white chiffon, which gave an exquisite frame to the face.

Sleeves are quite important this season, although there is no strict rule as to style. Elbow length ones still appear in "little frocks" of washing materials. Closely fitting long ones best become the hard-wearing dress which has to do duty for all kinds of out-of-doors occasions. Afternoon models show a bewildering variety . . . . the Magyar shape, which is graceful; the full Bishop shape, which is a little heavy unless the material be of the filmiest; the slashed sleeve, which naturally only appears on a period gown; and the double one, which seems to me rather unnecessary. Sleeves of three-quarter length are disappearing; long or short seems to be the ruling now.

Hat Lines.

I am afraid that hats in general are still going to be "amusing" rather than becoming to the majority of women. There are certain wearable shapes, notably the Cossack caps, the Renaissance bérets, and some of the new Breton sailors. Softly draped hats, like toques, lend a pleasant frame to some faces, and there are women who can carry off the postilion chapeau with success. Of all I like best the Renaissance beret. In soft velvet it is kind to the face and, moreover, it can be kept on the head without the help of a hand or an elastic band.

Colours.

As to colours which have been accepted, black—if this can be termed a colour—is easily first and naturally white is in demand with it. Also in the darker range come tones of brown, green and grey, with violet and some subdued red shades by way of change.

Printed materials are no longer in the lime-light. They were overdone very badly last season and are, therefore, more or less ignored by the really well-dressed woman. One or two little frocks of printed washing silk she may have in her wardrobe, but her more important gowns are made of plain fabrics which may, however, be hand embroidered or treated in one of the attractive ways already mentioned.

DIANA DANE.

" One of the most successful models shown at a recent collection was developed in black chiffon."

'Fashionable Information' from 'The Northern Whig' in 1935.

fashion flashes
Sensible Holiday Frocks.

All these styles may be tailored in cotton, "natural" linen, or fine rayons. Main feature of frock on the left is bold stripes in contrasting directions.

Centre frock is designed with full skirt and trim bodice above.

In this delightful frock, note the closely stitched design, and the wide, square-finish sleeves.

MANY of the frocks I have seen at recent fashion displays prove that summer clothes to-day are brighter than those we have seen for many years now. And they are sensible, too. A holiday frock loses neither its attraction nor its usefulness when the return home is made.

COTTON, linen and fine rayon are used for the majority of styles now available.

Pastel shades for the 'teenage, stripes and gay prints for the "twenties", and attractive single colour frocks for the not-so-young are being produced to meet the fairly heavy demand to-day.

I have sketched three styles that were shown at a fashion parade last week; one pastel shaded linen frock for the 'teenage girl with full skirt and trim bodice, a striped frock for the young woman in her twenties (note the contrasting runs of the stripes). and a delightful frock with closely stitched decoration for the woman over thirty.

(NORTHERN WHIG, 7 July 1947)

1942 – bridal party at the wedding of Miss Miriam O'Neill and Mr Alec West. The bridesmaid, Miss Doreen McDowell, later married Mr Matthew Turkington and, seven years later, became the mother of Hazel Turkington, Women's Editor of the 'Belfast Telegraph'.

Taking off again into the 1940s, the glamour is less apparent. War has been declared, and with it clothes rationing. With a suit worth 18 coupons and a dress 11, your 40 coupons don't go very far.

Suits are practical, still tweed, large shoulders and a very definite fitted waistline.

Silk stockings have been banned because of the war effort, so Sandie gives the audience a bit of a giggle in her grey wool hardy shift and a nothing of a felt hat — it's those little red ankle socks that keep out the cold.

But there is room for a little frivolity. Kissy looks adorable in her black shiny evening dress of thick satin, with that beautiful wide white collar skimming the neckline.

Sylvia is wearing a daring backless dress with shoestring straps (yes, they're still with us) and a great bow falling in bright red spotted silk gives a lovely detail to look at as she walks away.

Wedding dresses are few and far between, most of our models being married in the little two-piece with the nonsensical hat. However this one is pretty spectacular. The halter neckline has arrived — slipper satin, with a not-so-full skirt and a tiny bolero to cover the shoulders. The head-dress is almost a garland of tiny pink roses, worn here with a long white net veil.

RATIONING
of Clothing, Cloth, Foot-wear *and* Knitting-Wool has begun.

Since last Sunday, June 1st, cloth, clothes, boots, shoes and knitting-wool are rationed. A list of rationed goods, with the number of coupons they require has been published in the newspapers.

The new arrangements will take a few days to settle down. Meantime you will lose nothing by postponing your purchases. Shops will have their usual supplies, *and* NO ONE *will be able to buy more than* YOU *are entitled to.*

ANSWERS TO QUESTIONS WH[ICH ARE] PUZZLING YOU

Shall I be better or worse off with my ration?

The Government have been asking you to save, and at the same time have had to restrict the making and importing of many goods. The rationing of clothes and footwear *does not mean* a further restriction. It means "fair shares" of what there is. There is less to buy than in peace time, but within your ration you can buy and wear whatever you choose.

What about orders given before June 1st?

As a general rule these will require coupons but goods that are being specially made for you will not require coupons *if they are delivered before 14th June and the maker has written evidence of having received the order before 1st June.*

Should I keep my current Food Book when I get the new one?

Yes. You will want it so long as there are unused "margarine" clothing coupons in it. You will be told how to get a new Clothing Coupon Card afterwards.

Where an[d] can I use [my coupons?]

At any [...] registrat[...]

Won't [...] clothes [...]

No[...] cou[...] for t[...] curr[...] ove[...] an[...] th[...] wi[...] fo[...]

NUMBER OF COUPONS NEEDED

Men and Boys	Adult	Child	Women and Girls	Adult	Child
Unlined mackintosh or cape	9	7	Lined mackintoshes, or coats (over 28 in. in length)	14	11
Other mackintoshes, or raincoat, or overcoat	16	11	Jacket, or short coat (under 28 in. in length)	11	8
Coat, or jacket, or blazer or like garment	13	8	Dress, or gown, or frock—woollen	11	8
Waistcoat, or pull-over, or cardigan, or jersey	5	3	Dress, or gown, or frock—other material	7	5
Trousers (other than fustian or corduroy)	8	6	Gym tunic, or girl's skirt with bodice	8	6
Fustian or corduroy trousers	5	5	Blouse, or sports shirt, or cardigan, or jumper	5	3
Shorts	5	3	Skirt, or divided skirt	7	5
Overalls, or dungarees or like garment	6	4	Overalls, or dungarees or like garment	6	4
Dressing-gown or bathing-gown	8	6	Apron, or pinafore	3	2
Night-shirt or pair of pyjamas	8	6	Pyjamas	8	6
Shirt, or combinations—woollen	8	6	Nightdress	6	5
Shirt, or combinations—other material	5	4	Petticoat, or slip, or combination, or cami-knickers	4	3
Pants, or vest, or bathing costume, or child's blouse	4	2	Other undergarments, including corsets	3	2
Pair of socks or stockings	3	1	Pair of stockings	2	1
Collar, or tie, or pair of cuffs	1	1	Pair of socks (ankle length)	1	1
Two handkerchiefs	1	1	Collar, or tie, or pair of cuffs	1	1
Scarf, or pair of gloves or mittens	2	2	Two handkerchiefs	1	1
Pair of slippers or goloshes	4	2	Scarf, or pair of gloves or mittens or muff	2	2
Pair of boots or shoes	7	3	Pair of slippers, boots or shoes	5	3
[...] aiters or spats	3	1			

[...]er yard depend on the width. For example, a yard of woollen cloth [...] oupons. The same amount of cotton or other cloth needs 2 coupons. [...] KNITTING WOOL. 1 coupon for two ounces.

[...] MAY BE BOUGHT *WITHOUT* COUPONS

[...] sizes generally suitable for infants less than 4 years old. ¶ Boiler suits [...]ace overalls. ¶ Hats and caps. ¶ Sewing thread. ¶ Mending wool and [...] shoe laces. ¶ Tapes, braids, ribbons and other fabrics of 3 inches or less [...]ce and lace net. ¶ Sanitary towels. ¶ Braces, suspenders and garters. [...]logs. ¶ Black-out cloth dyed black. ¶ All second-hand articles.

[Noti]ce to Retailers

[...]owed to get fresh stocks of cloth up to and including June 28th, of [...] up to and including June 21st, WITHOUT SURRENDERING [...]se dates they will be able to obtain fresh stocks only by turning in [...]s. Steps have been taken, in the interests of the smaller retailers, to [...]ods the quantity of goods which can be supplied by a wholesaler or [...] retailer however large his orders. *Further information can be obtained* [...]isations.

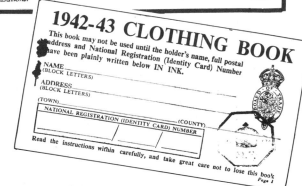
1942-43 CLOTHING BOOK

This book may not be used until the holder's name, full postal address and National Registration (Identity Card) Number have been plainly written below IN INK.

NAME (BLOCK LETTERS)

ADDRESS (BLOCK LETTERS)

(TOWN)

NATIONAL REGISTRATION (IDENTITY CARD) NUMBER   (COUNTY)

Read the instructions within carefully, and take great care not to lose this book

Page 1

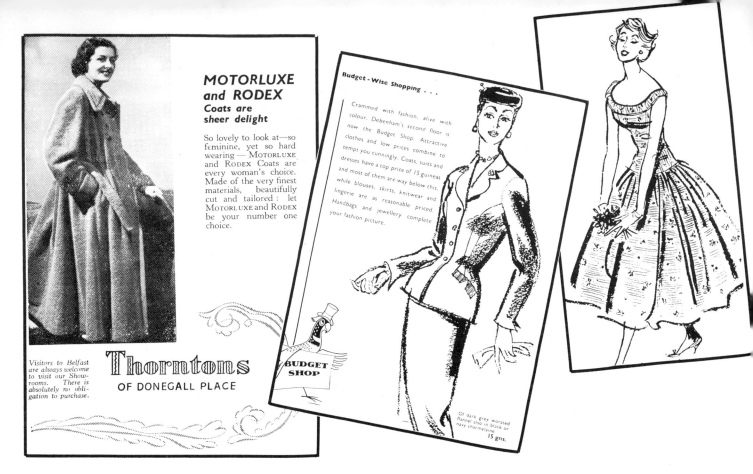

MOTORLUXE and RODEX

Coats are sheer delight

So lovely to look at—so feminine, yet so hard wearing — MOTORLUXE and RODEX Coats are every woman's choice. Made of the very finest materials, beautifully cut and tailored : let MOTORLUXE and RODEX be your number one choice.

Visitors to Belfast are always welcome to visit our Show-rooms. There is absolutely no obli-gation to purchase.

Thorntons

OF DONEGALL PLACE

Budget - Wise Shopping . . .

Crammed with fashion, alive with colour, Debenham's second floor is now the Budget Shop. Attractive clothes and low prices combine to tempt you cunningly. Coats, suits and dresses have a top price of 15 guineas and most of them are way below this, while blouses, skirts, knitwear and lingerie are as reasonable priced. Handbags and jewellery complete your fashion picture.

BUDGET SHOP

Of dark grey worsted flannel also in black or navy charmelaine
15 gns.

And here we are in the Fifties at last. The war is over and it's goodbye to austerity. Annie is showing us Christian Dior's 'New Look'. Her dress is bottle-green – soft shoulders, wasp waist, bosom padded for extra curve, and yards and yards of material for the panelled skirt; all teamed with silk (Ah, bliss!) stockings and high, pointed shoes.

Sally obviously loves her trapeze-line outfit. Note the squared shoulder box-like shape, all in softest pale pink jersey.

Sandie prefers the A-line look – soft black sleeveless top and an A-line skirt that comes to just above the knee.

Greta's make-up is stunning: black lines drawn round the eyes to give a feline air; heavy black eyebrows pencilled in sooty black. The Chanel suit is still with us, this time in cream bouclé wool trimmed with heavy chocolate-brown braid on the collar and down the front of the jacket. Her skirt is pencil slim.

Heather, the bride, makes her final entrance in white shantung, the skirt full, tight waist clasped in a cummerbund, the collar a discreet polo neck line. Her hair is scraped back into a topknot, with a twinkling tiara surrounding it.

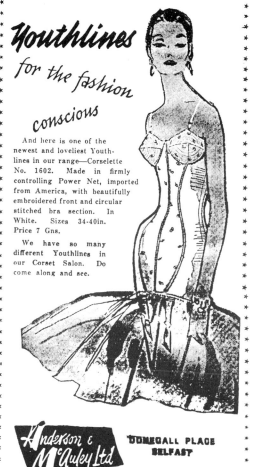

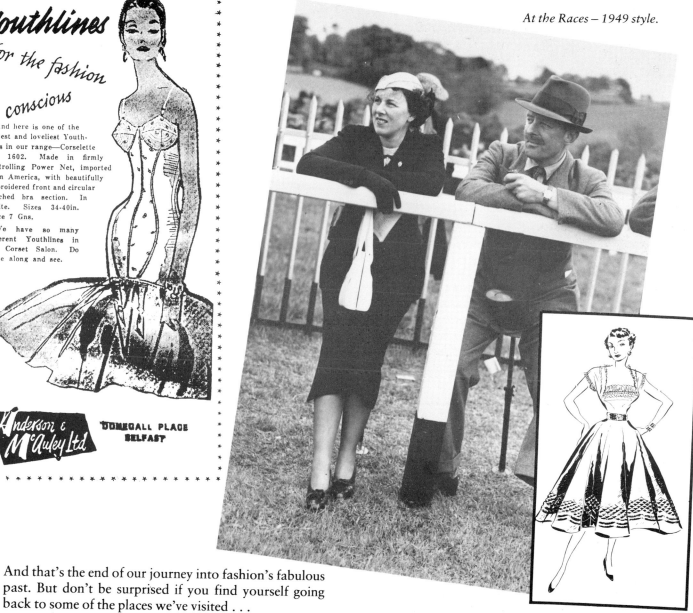

At the Races – 1949 style.

And that's the end of our journey into fashion's fabulous past. But don't be surprised if you find yourself going back to some of the places we've visited . . .

Brendan Colgan

Brendan Colgan retired as Headmaster of St Mary's Primary School in Belfast last year. But he is much more than simply a retired teacher. He is a writer, a local historian, and an authority on children's games. Many of the street games played by children today have evolved over generations. And the process of evolution is an endless one. In his book 'Let's Play' Brendan takes a detailed look at how those games are played by today's children. In looking back and contrasting schools of the past in both town and country, Brendan reveals much of the warmth of his own personality and of his own personal philosophy – the art of acknowledging others with affection and respect.

Our wee School

Our wee school's a good wee school,
It's made of bricks and plaster;
The only thing that's wrong with it
Is our wee baldy master.
He goes to the pub on Saturday night,
He goes to church on Sunday,
He asks the Lord to give him strength
To slaughter us on Monday.

How we loved listening to Rose, a friend of the family, singing that song when she came down from Belfast to visit our house in Glenloughan, a townland near Kilkeel in County Down. We were only youngsters then in 1939 and Rose was nearly twenty. She often made the journey from Belfast to Kilkeel but it was a few years later before I realised why she was such a faithful visitor. The reason – she had met and fallen in love with Stephen from County Fermanagh who was then working at stone quarrying in Mourne.

Rose and Stephen would spend many an evening ceilidhing in our house and there'd be fun and stories galore. But if we were to be part of it all we had to make sure we had our 'home exercises' done for Miss Gertie, Miss Sloan or Master Dawson, our teachers in Star of the Sea Public Elementary School. Naturally the talk and stories were often about school and schooling, and of one thing Rose and Stephen were both certain, going to school in 1939 seemed very much easier than they had

known it. And then the reminiscing and storytelling would begin, with Rose often singing street songs and rhymes which she had learnt during her years at school in Belfast. Along with the rest of us, Stephen enjoyed hearing about the large Boys' and Girls' School which Rose had attended, because his school had been small and thatched, tucked away in County Fermanagh.

I'll always remember Stephen telling us that he lived on the Bog Road, and his description of the mist rising from the bogs as he made his way to school carrying his few school books, a small farl of buttered griddle bread, and a piece of turf, for the master often warned: 'No turf, no fire'!

The master would always be waiting at the door as his pupils, half wearing clogs, half in their bare feet, arrived for nine o'clock each morning. All forty, Protestant and Catholic, were taught by him, for he was the school's sole teacher. He allowed them no time for dilly-dallying. The turf was left outside in the turf shed near the dry toilets, which always had a dreadful smell. Within a few minutes, having hung up their coats at the back of the classroom, some made their way to sit at the wooden two-seater desks. There were not enough desks for everyone in the one classroom which was the entire school, so those 'for reading' stood up near the open fire which was always glowing. When this group or class had finished its reading lesson, it sat down and another took its place. Often when Stephen was in the reading group he would look over at the big roll-book which remained open on the master's desk where they stood.

Mornings were an uneasy time for the pupils. If they saw that the master's cheeks were a bright red colour he was sure to be tough on them that day. Without a word being said, they knew that he had had a 'drop of whiskey' before leaving home. Woe betide the pupil who gave trouble, and that would also go for any parents coming with a complaint, or asking for a pupil to get out early to help with the hay or potatoes.

Stephen loved and respected the master, for the subjects he taught were always interesting. But the master also received help in his teaching from the boys and girls in Standard Six and Seven. Often Stephen himself took the reading lesson while another pupil, usually a girl, would be busily engaged helping some of the younger children learn to write. This senior pupil held the hand of each of the young ones in turn, guiding them as they held the chalk and copied the letters of the alphabet onto their slates. Later they would write unaided with a pen and ink in their exercise books. Geography, poetry, geometry and religious instruction were among the wide range of subjects taught. Religious instruction began each day at 3 o'clock but it was only for the Catholic pupils. Needless to say they weren't too happy at having to stay in until about half past three for this subject when the Protestants could go home at three o'clock!

For Stephen, thinking about heaven during the RI class was often thinking about the fun he would have going home from school. There were hedges to be jumped over to see who could leap the highest or the longest. Maybe they'd go to the shop for pokes of sweets, and stone somebody's hens on the way! Climbing to the top of haystacks and sliding down again was another favourite home-going pastime, but if the farmer caught them there was trouble and the culprits knew what to expect. Paddling in the river, catching stickle-backs . . . the fun was never ending.

But it all ended when the boys and girls reached their

homes. After a good healthy meal of perhaps potatoes, bacon and cabbage, and a mug of buttermilk, there was work for them to be done around the house and farm. Indeed Stephen was certain that he and all the other boys leaving school at Standard Seven or Eight were already experienced farmers. However, since his father's farm was too small to support his family, he had to seek work elsewhere. Now he was in Mourne, had met Rose and along with the rest of us had learned from her songs like 'The Doffin' Mistress' and 'Green Peas and Barley-O', songs which were so much a part of her schooldays in Belfast. We loved it when she sometimes taught us the games and rhymes she had played in her school yard, or in the streets nearby.

Unlike Stephen's school, Rose's was a high building with the girls upstairs and the boys downstairs. There were separate entrance doors and separate playgrounds for each school. The Girls' school consisted of two large rooms and the 'baby' room. In the 'baby' room there were eight rows of seats, each row higher than the one in front of it, in gallery formation. On the little remaining floor space was the teacher's desk and chair with the blackboard on the wall behind her. The two other rooms held the older pupils and all three rooms were crowded. There were not enough desks and like Stephen's school one class had to stand if another was writing, perhaps in their *Vere Foster Copy Books,* or taking something down from the blackboard in their jotters or exercise books. Cursive writing was used from the pupils' earliest days, initially using chalk and slates, then pencils and pens as they progressed through the school.

A monitoress usually helped the four teachers with their work and this young girl must surely have been sorely needed. Rose remembered that when she was in Standard Four there were seventy-eight pupils in her class. The large globe of the world in the senior room fascinated her but it was scarcely ever used, as the main subjects were the legendary '3 Rs' – reading, writing and arithmetic. Cookery on Wednesday afternoons was every

Brackney Primary School in the Mournes, one of the many elementary schools whose doors are now closed forever.

girl's favourite subject. It was taught in the classroom where the gas stove was kept for making the teacher's tea. In pairs the senior girls brought in to the school the shared ingredients for the dish to be cooked that day. These same girls divided the cake or buns when they were baked and ready to be brought home. Rose often told us about the Wednesday when she and her partner had to wait a long time on their turn for the oven and so kept beating the cake mixture. But their patience was rewarded for their sandwich was the highest of all baked that day. Soda bread, wheaten bread, apple tarts and rice pudding were Rose's cookery teachers' favourites in the cookery classes.

Like Stephen, Rose loved the fun in the 'play yard' and when going home from school in the evenings. They played and played. There were ring games like 'Kneeling on the Carpet', 'There's a Wee Girl in Our Class', and 'Wallflower'. Skipping games like 'Nelson in the Army', 'Eightsy-Datesy', 'My Aunt Jane', and 'Skinny Malink Melodian Legs'. There were ball games, partner games and group games. Rose introduced us to hop-scotch and told us boys the names of games of marbles her brothers played in the school yard and on the pavements near school.

The fun, happiness and abandonment surrounding life for Rose and her friends at the Public Elementary School in many ways made the financial and social harshness of life somewhat easier for them to bear. Poverty and un-

HERE WE DANCE LOOBY LOO

I put my right hand in, I put my right hand out, I give my right hand a shake, shake, shake, And turn my-self a-bout! Here we dance loo-by loo, Here we dance loo-by light, Here we dance loo-by loo, Ev-'ry Sat-ur-day night.

"Here we dance looby loo,
Here we dance looby light,
Here we dance looby loo,
Every Saturday night."

'My Aunt Jane'

My Aunt Jane, she called me in,
She gave me tea out of her wee tin.
Half a bap and sugar on the top
And three black lumps out of her wee shop.

Skinny-Malink

Skinny Malink melodian legs
Big banana feet
Went to the pictures
And couldn't get a seat.
When she got a seat
She fell fast asleep.
Skinny Malink melodian legs,
Big banana feet.

'Eightsy Datesy'

Eightsy datesy miss the rope you're out-e-o.
If you had been where I had been
You wouldn't have been put out-e-o.
All the boys and girls
People out of work-e-o.
Eightsy datesy miss the rope you're out-e-o.

'Did You Ever'

Did you ever ever ever
In your long-legged life
See a long-legged man
With a long-legged wife.

No I never never never
In my long-legged life
Seen a long-legged man
With a long-legged wife.

'The Wind, The Wind'

The wind, the wind,
The wind blew high;
The rain came scattering from the sky.
Mary Shiels says she'll die
If she doesn't get the fellow with the rosy eye.
She is handsome, she is pretty,
She is the girl from Belfast city.
She's a courting one, two, three
Please won't you tell me who is she.

Pupils of the Star of the Sea Public Elementary School in 1948. Brendan Colgan is in the back row, at the extreme right.

employment were part of the fabric of family life of so many of Rose's young school companions.

Most mothers were in the nearby spinning mills, working long wearying hours as doffers, spinners, weavers or in the reeling rooms. Indeed it was to seek and luckily gain employment in the reeling room of a local mill where her mother worked that Rose left school when she was thirteen years and three months. How easily the song 'The Doffin' Mistress' came to her lips when she sang for us at night.

But in Glenloughan we couldn't understand the meaning of the song and it was never sung in our school or yard. Miss Lucy Bartley, who took us for singing while playing the harmonium, preferred songs like 'The Lark in the Clear Air', 'Danny Boy', and 'Bless this House'. Besides teaching these beautiful songs, Miss Bartley introduced the senior pupils to the rudiments of music. Each subject in turn was comprehensively taught throughout the school. During English class, poetry was Master Dawson's great love and it was always his wish to share that love with us. Wordsworth, Keats, Padraic Colum were poets whose works were very familiar to us at the age of eleven or twelve. Geometry, algebra, geography, drawing, needlework and cookery were among the range of subjects taught to the older children of Star of the Sea in the early 1940s. Adequate seating, good reading and writing materials and a happy learning atmosphere perhaps reflected the quiet development of Public Elementary Education in those years.

No school vacations were more popular than the 'potato holidays' when we could earn money gathering potatoes for the local farmers or even at home. There was also money to be earned in the autumn when the blackberries were ripe on the hedges. After school, carrying a can or bucket, we set off to gather the berries. When the containers were full we brought them to Johnny Magee's shop. Johnny weighed the berries and having satisfied himself that we hadn't added any water or pebbles to increase their weight, he paid us. We were

Classroom scene from an old primer.

proud of that money which was often carefully 'put past' to buy shoes or boots for the winter. We needed this footwear, for the pupils of Star of the Sea walked many a mile during their youth, like walking the two miles to Confession to Massforth every second Saturday of the month.

On the way we called at different houses for a drink of water. One house always held a special kind of fear for us and we didn't ever call there. The owner was Charlie Annett and he had a wooden leg, having been severely wounded during heavy fighting at the Front in the First World War. We were convinced that if we gave him any trouble he would promptly screw off his leg and hit the first one of us he could catch with it. How wrong we were! We later learned that Charlie Annett was a quiet, good man – a victim of the dreadful 1914–18 war.

Now in 1941 another World War was raging, but for us in the Star of the Sea school in the quiet Mourne country, it all seemed so far away. We had heard about bombings and blackouts, had seen ration books and identity cards and had been given gas masks in school. Even though a small airfield for the US Air Force had been built a few miles away at Cranfield, the things of war meant very little to us. We attended school and enjoyed the fun which always seemed to be part of our lives in the classroom.

Suddenly one morning Rose and Stephen, now married, hurriedly left for Belfast. Rose had just learned that her brother had been killed in an air raid in England. Terror was soon to strike in Belfast on Easter Tuesday 1941. The dreadful reality and agony of what was now happening there became clearer in our young minds as we saw the evacuees arrive to fill houses, halls, schools and empty dwelling houses in Mourne.

Some of the families and children who had come to live and attend school with us stayed only a short time, while others remained longer. Indeed there were many who found themselves a future husband or wife as a result of having been evacuated from one place to another. In this respect Mourne was no exception.

It was indeed a time of change for the children of Northern Ireland. As the war ended they were experiencing quiet developments in the curriculum and in methods of teaching. The title 'Primary' would soon replace 'Public Elementary'.

But for my pals and myself a completely new world lay ahead, education at secondary school. My first days as a boarder in a Belfast College in 1945 were strange and lonely. Here was a completely different world of learning, a world of languages, mathematics, science and Shakespeare. However, like all entering secondary education I was soon to realise that it was a world for which our teachers had been diligently preparing us during our happy, carefree days at Public Elementary School.

114

THE LITTLE EVACUEES WON'T STARVE

ELABORATE PROVISION

MADE FOR THEIR WELFARE

STATIONS AS RESTAURANTS

PARENTS OF BELFAST SCHOOLCHILDREN NEED HAVE NO FEAR THAT THEIR OFFSPRING WILL SUFFER FROM HUNGER ON THE JOURNEY TO THEIR NEW HOMES IN THE BIG EVACUATION FROM THE CITY.

Plans for their welfare in this direction were made some time ago, and this morning at the three railway stations these were started upon. Seldom, if ever, have the catering branches faced such a huge order.

30,000 CHILDREN TO GO.

To-morrow and Monday 30,000 children are being evacuated, 12,000 each from the Great Northern Railway Station and the L M S Station, and 6,000 from the Belfast and Co. Down Railway Station.

Ten children and one teacher will be allocated to each compartment, and when they take their seats Boy Scout volunteers will hand to each teacher the following ration for each child:

HALF-PINT CARTON OF MILK.
TWO HAM SANDWICHES.
A BUN.
AN APPLE.
TWO STICKS OF BARLEY SUGAR.

Belfast evacuees Sidney and Don Smyth, and Alex Hamilton at the GNR station, in readiness for their journey to Cookstown. All the children set off with labels pinned to their coats in case they got lost.

Winifred Doran

Winifred Doran's love of growing and using herbs is something which she can always remember. It is something which she inherited from a remarkable old lady, her Great Aunt Gertrude. The world which Winifred remembers as a small girl was a very different place from the world of today. Perhaps it was a more suitable place to reflect on the peace and tranquility associated with traditional herbs and their associated remedies, but just as her Great Aunt did in the Twenties and Thirties, today Winifred Doran insists that no garden is complete without at least a small corner reserved for her favourite plants. One day Winifred wrote to Gloria Hunniford offering her a short talk on roses. Soon she was a regular contributor first on 'A Taste of Hunni' and latterly on 'Day by Day'.

Down Memory Lane

It is more than half a century ago since my Aunt Gertrude and I walked through the doorway which led from her main garden into the extra-fragrant, walled domain of her herb, fruit and shrub garden. Looking back at it now, it seems that it was always summer and the days were always long.

The first time that I went through that doorway as a small girl I reached out to close the door after me. In those far-off days children were trained to be 'good-mannered'. And closing the door after you was a sign that your training had not been in vain. I can still hear my Aunt Gertrude. 'Darling,' she said quietly, 'this is a door that we never close. This garden is filled with God's Peace. And we must let that Peace escape and fly out all round the world.' From that moment a herb-garden spelt joy to me. I was hooked for ever-more on these beautiful, fragrant plants which exude Peace and Happiness.

My Aunt Gertrude was a little woman with twinkling blue eyes, snow-white hair, and that high-spirited quality that makes *everything* fresh every day. She laughed a lot and I recall her laughter when we were talking about making your face beautiful with make-up when she was young. 'There were only two sorts of face-powder then,' she laughed, 'white and pink, and no nice girl used either.' We children always felt happy and secure in her presence. She was such fun, so knowledgeable, so full of warmth and kindness and so interested in all our doings, that we loved her dearly.

She was dedicated to her garden and to all humanity. Her philosophy of life was a simple one. She believed that to be happy you only needed to reflect on the wisdom of the Creation and obey the rules of Nature. She was much interested in the advances made in the medical world of her day, which resulted in the saving of lives. But she exhorted everyone to make and use a herb-garden, even if only on a yard or balcony. For, she said, by using herbs, with common sense, in cooking and healing, you could prevent ills from ever 'taking-off' in the first place. She used to say that herbs did so much for the blood, nervous system and digestion that people forgot to be ill. But if anyone did complain of a pain of any sort, even the plain old heartache of adolescence, she had a herbal cure at hand.

She would produce one of her herbal concoctions, with the statement, 'Sure you won't know yourself after a drop of this.' Then she would take you for a stroll round her aromatic garden, picking the herbs for you to sniff as you poured out your woes into her sympathetic ear. After that she would set you down to a good meal which owed its deliciousness to her clever use of herbs. By which time your ills were cured and your troubles were forgotten. You *truly* did not indeed know yourself.

Dear Aunt Gertrude. Her world was as far away from ours as the North Pole is from the South. Widowed while young, she lived in a big old country house with a housekeeper who was devoted to her. She had a gardener

THE HERB GARDEN

"It is a commodious and a pleasant thyng to a mansion to have an orcherde of sundry fruites; but it is more commodious to have a fayre garden repleted with herbs of aromatyek and redolent savours." — Andrew Borde.

Little more than a hundred years ago the herb-garden was a necessary part of the housewife's domain. In earlier times still it was known as a physic garden, and every wife had her still-room and was expected to supply her household with home-brewed potions, poultices, cosmetics, preserves and wines. The country housewife to-day, unless she was brought up by a grandmother versed in the properties of plants, would hesitate to trust to the old simples, many of which were indeed very good. There is no reason, however, why she should not grow culinary herbs other than the familiar mint, sage and parsley. Rissoles, stews, sauces and fish are often very dull, but delicious flavours can result from the judicious use of fresh, chopped herbs. French cooks have long realised that well-flavoured food is the most easily digested.

Here are some herbs which can be grown with little trouble, either sown from seed, obtained from cuttings, or ordered from a good nursery gardener. They are best grown in long narrow beds with paving between them, so that all may be easily reached dry-shod, even on damp days. A herb garden can be very attractive, many of the flowers are charming, and the leaves many shades of green. Few people, for instance, realise the beauty of parsley as an edging.

Chives.—Much milder than onion. Spikes only eaten. Bluish flowers. **Tarragon.**—Needs sun, for home-made vinegar and Tartare Sauce. **Fennel.**—For Fish. Tall, graceful plant. **Sorrel** (Rumex).—Good for soups. Spreads rather too rapidly. **Lemon Thyme** (Thymus citriodorus).—Grow this as well as Common Thyme. **Winter Savoury, Summer Savoury.**—For flavouring sausages, broad beans, etc. **Sweet Marjoram.**—All kinds of flavouring. Very effective grown in large masses. **Sweet Green Basil.**—For sauces and soups. **Chervil.**—Gather when leaves 3-4in. high. Mild flavour. Soups and salads. **Chicory.**—Sow June for leaves for winter salads. Dislikes being moved. **Borage.**—Leaves for claret and other cups. Deep blue flowers. **Coriander.**—Seeds used in curry. **Carraway.**—Seeds used to flavour cheese, soups, bread and cakes. **Celery.**—For salads. Allow some to seed, for use in soups and curries. **Nasturtium.**—Seeds may be pickled like capers. Leaves and petals for salads. **Dill.**—Spicy taste. Leaves may be added to fish, or pickled cucumber. **Lemon Mint,** as well as **Spear Mint.**—Leaves may be candied. **Marigold.**—A few petals in soups and puddings. Bitter. **Tansey.**—Puddings and cakes. Very bitter. **Camomile.**—Dry yellow disks for tea. A good tonic. **Bay.**—For sauces, soups and milk puddings.

Annuals.—Sow in May, tradition says when the moon is waxing.

Perennials.—Should be transplanted every three years, or given a top dressing of rich soil.

Gathering, drying and storing.—Gather on a dry day when just beginning to flower. Dry either in a shady, airy place or in a hot oven. Crumble and pour into bottles, cork tightly and label.

Mixed herbs.—Equal quantities of dried parsley, thyme, marjoram, winter savoury, half quantity sweet basil; some dried, grated lemon rind; six dry bay leaves, some celery seeds. Grate rind and dry in oven. Pound celery seeds. Mix all herbs thoroughly, pound again. Store in bottles. For use: put half teaspoonful in muslin. Excellent flavour.

Modagaxan periwinkle, Vinca rosea

Feverfew

who came faithfully every day to help her with her large garden. He grew old in her service and loved the garden as dearly as she did. (That beautiful old home has long since been demolished to make way for a motorway.) In her day that motorway was a winding country road where the farm carts and haywains ambled quietly along. Nobody was in a hurry. In summer the hedgrows were fragrant with wild roses, honeysuckle, hawthorn and elder flower, and in autumn they were scarlet with berries. Many a time I helped my aunt to pick these for wine-making and other delights.

Thinking of her now fills me with wonder. For this woman, born on a farm in the Victorian era and living for nearly a hundred years (until after the Second World War) was able to preserve the values and some of the customs of her own youth. Her mind never became rigid,

nor indeed did her body. She was able to adjust to all the changing customs that, inevitably, came with the passing years. When anyone commented on this quality she used to laugh and say: 'It's the herbs I use. We can all stay youthful with herbs.'

When the First World War ended, my aunt and her contemporaries had to adjust to a new lifestyle. The cost of the war was depleting everybody. Auntie was brought up in Victorian solidity, where change was unheard of. A man who worked on her land before the war earned a weekly wage of about £2. On this he could raise a family comfortably. His home was lit with oil lamps. He paid no income-tax nor rates, and his rent was about 5/- (25p) a week. His family ate well, for a joint of beef cost 10 old pennies (4¼p) per lb. He could even go into a general store and test his eyes himself and buy a pair of spectacles for 1/-. And he had his weekly bath in a zinc tub in front of the fire, then trimmed his corns with a cut-throat razor. No chiropodists then!

The revolution in society after the war must have been shattering for the older generation, though they must have seen the Twenties as full of promise of that land fit

SPRING-CLEANING.

There are many differences of opinion as to when spring-cleaning should commence. Some do it early to get it over before the warm weather, which renders the work more trying, but the disadvantages of doing it at that time are many. First of all, it is desirable to wait till most of the fires are out for the summer before starting to clean. Some say, of course, that in our climate we always have fires; granted, but less constantly in summer than in winter. Moreover, when the weather is fine, all kinds of bedding may be hung out for drying or sunning. Winter curtains can well be aired out of doors before putting them away for the summer. Floors dry more quickly in the late spring, and the hot sun pouring in through open windows both disinfects and purifies the dismantled rooms.

It is an old saying and a true one that everything is easy when you know the way. This particularly applies to spring-cleaning, and the first piece of advice I would give is—Prepare. Don't just say on Sunday night, "I think I'll start spring-cleaning to-morrow". It can't be done in this haphazard fashion, and rushing it is a false economy. You know when the sweep is coming. Be ready for him. Have all your cleaning utensils and preparations ready before the actual cleaning begins. The latter can be made weeks before, so that, when the time for the big effort comes, you can go right ahead.

Then, having made your house spick and span, the welfare of its inhabitants once again is the object of your attention.

This is the season for preserving and storing eggs.

In these days of small houses and resultant cramped pantry accommodation, storing eggs in crocks is rather a problem. The preservative "Oteg" solves this, since once the eggs are thoroughly dry, after simply being dipped in the liquid, they can be stored in any room that is not too hot, in baskets, boxes, dress boxes, etc.; moreover, they *can* be boiled and they whip splendidly. One of our readers, having been recommended by this magazine to use "Oteg", has written to us declaring that it is a wonderful preservative, and that she now uses no other.

Store places for eggs or for any other foodstuffs should be well ventilated. If cupboards are air-tight, they should have a few holes drilled in the doors, a little copper gauze nailed to the inside excluding dust.

While on the subject of food, the point arises : What are you going to do about the preparation of a meal while you are busy turning out rooms? Clearly something which can be put in the oven and left will be the most convenient. I would suggest Irish Stew made in a Phoenix casserole dish, or here is a suitable fish recipe which is tasty and quick.

Roll one fillet of fish for each person, and place in a well-buttered Phoenix dish. Cover with tomato or white sauce, flavoured with lemon, or anchovy. Cook for 30 minutes.

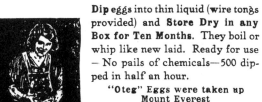
THE CLEANING OF WOOD.

Painted Wood, Unvarnished.

Preparations : Have soft woollen cloths. Dissolve some borax, and add it to a bucket of lukewarm water. Have a basin of clean lukewarm water near at hand.

Method : Start at the lowest point and wash upward, so that the dirty water will not trickle down. Wet a small surface at a time, then wash it, using soap and flannel. For very dirty parts, such as the low part of doors and window ledges, a very soft brush may be used, but never a stiff scrubbing brush, as this would remove both paint and dirt. Rinse with clean lukewarm water as you wash, and dry as well as possible.

The 'Ulster Countrywoman'

The small figure in white standing on the footpath is me – Winifred Doran – in the Twenties!

for heroes to live in, which they aimed to build. We children were carefree and happy. We were able to play in the quiet avenues and streets, for the traffic was mostly horse-drawn and slow. The trams rattled along the main roads on their lines (an adult paid one old penny for a long journey) and now and then a motor-car would 'speed' along at ten or fifteen miles an hour – a reason to stop playing and stare. We trundled hoops, became experts with a skipping rope, played rounders (a ball game which involved a lot of running all over the road), marbles, and we competed with each other at spinning tops (we called them 'peeries'). We had different seasons for the different games. Games where we danced round in

a ring, singing, were popular – 'The Farmer wants a Wife', 'Green Gravel Green Gravel', 'Down on the Carpet' come back to memory. No one disturbed us. But most of these have vanished long since and those happy carefree days have rushed away all too quickly.

While my aunt tended and distributed her herbs and her happiness those Twenties' children had become the young adults of the Thirties. Life was still gathering speed. Despite a world-wide depression and much unemployment, enthusiasm and hope persisted. Now it was the day of the dance-hall and the tennis-club. Hiking became a popular keep-fit exercise, as did cycling. Young people did not go to pubs then. We gathered in the

121

Before the war, shops were much more inclined to display their wares on the pavement, as this scene on Belfast's Newtownards Road indicates.

confectioner's to drink lemonade, while we all pontificated on how to bring about all the reforms the country needed. Entertainments were cheap in the Thirties.

You could have three hours entertainment in the cinema for six or eight old pennies. You could arrange a supper-dance at Albert White's Ball-room for 2/6 per person, and you could accumulate a lot of shopping at Woolworth's where 'there was nothing over sixpence'.

Glamour became the key word of the Thirties and everyone was trying to imitate the glamourous film stars. Fashion became romantic again. The wireless progressed from the cat's whisker and headphones period (where a door slammed would wreck everything by dislodging the cat's whisker). The valve set with speakers arrived and we all became (without realising it) university students of the air. Desmond McCarthy talked about books. James Agate reviewed plays. Christopher Stone educated us musically with gramophone records. All who loved gardens never missed listening to our gardening expert – Mr Middleton. Soon, in unpretentious little Ulster, we began to imagine ourselves to be as knowledgeable as any who lived in the grand capitals of the world. And just a year or two before the darkness descended once more with the outbreak of the Second World War, there was the exciting talk of Television, which we could not believe could really come true. Of course, by this time, many people aspired to a motor-car. We bought ours in 1939. It was a Morris Minor, and cost us all of £100. Dear were the days.

So the Thirties drifted into the Forties, with the outbreak of war in 1939. Food was rationed (2 oz butter per person per week). We were issued with identity cards, ration books and gas-masks. Our loved ones marched off to war, many never to return. The war entered our civilian world as the enemy bombs rained down, killing thousands. Women who had given up careers in the Thirties upon marriage, now all marched back to work to help the war effort. And the seeds of Women's Lib were sown. Material prosperity returned as a result of the

124

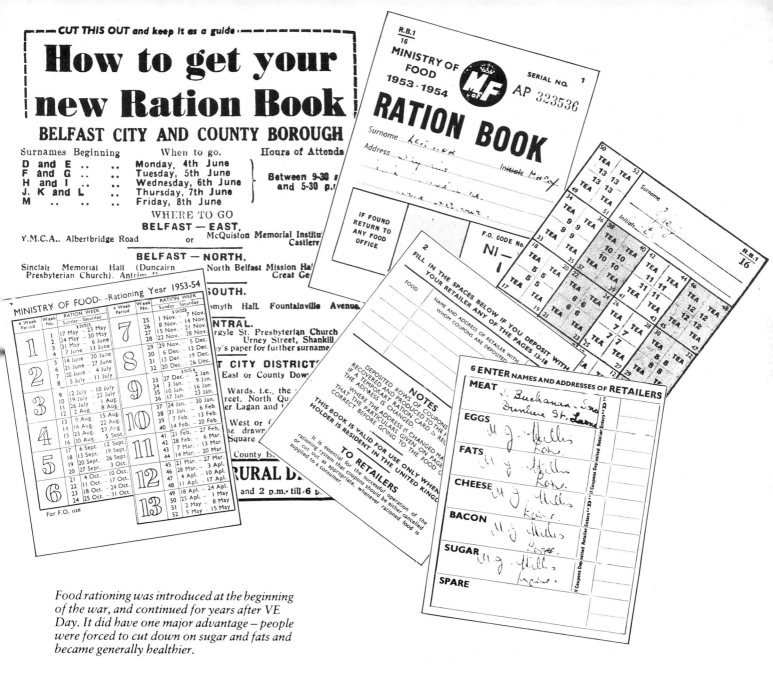

Food rationing was introduced at the beginning of the war, and continued for years after VE Day. It did have one major advantage – people were forced to cut down on sugar and fats and became generally healthier.

How to make RATIONS FOR ONE go f-u-r-t-h-e-r

Planning meals is usually easier with several ration books than with just one. But the woman (or man) living alone has this advantage, that she has only her own tastes to consider. The following suggestions show what can be done with a little ingenuity. Women who are alone during the day will also find these hints useful.

What to do when you have to take your meat ration as —

BREAST OF LAMB: Bone and remove surplus fat (rendering the fat down for dripping). Make a savoury stuffing, spread on the meat and roll up. Tie or skewer firmly. This can then be baked, roasted or braised. If it is roasted, cook slowly.

SCRAG END OF LAMB OR NECK OF VEAL: Use it for a stew or casserole with plenty of vegetables (leeks are very good) and some dried beans and peas. Use herbs for flavouring and a dash of vinegar from the pickle bottle.

PORK: Make it into a stew or casserole, using plenty of vegetables and some dried beans or peas. Or braise it on a bed of vegetables and serve pork sausages with it.

Suggestions for easily made main-meal dishes

MIXED GRILL
1 rasher of bacon, 1 sausage, a slice liver sausage, fried potato and peas or beans.

SARDINE AND EGG SCRAMBLE: 1 small knob of fat; ½ small leek, chopped finely; 1½ level tablespoons dried egg, re-constituted; 1 level tablespoon chopped parsley; salt, pepper, and pinch of mustard; 2 teaspoons vinegar; 3 sardines.

Fry leek in fat, add egg, seasoning and parsley, and scramble in usual way. Mash sardines with vinegar, add to egg and mix well.

POINTS CHANGES
For four-week period No. 11 April 29th to May 26th

UP—CANNED LUNCHEON MEATS—6 lb. from 86 to 129; 4 lb. from 57 to 86; 3 lb. from 43 to 64; 2½ lb. from 35 to 52; 1 lb. from 15 to 22; 12 oz. from 11 to 17; any other size or sliced from 16 to 24 points per lb.
CANNED BEANS (in Tomato or Vegetable Sauce). A1 or 16 oz. from 3 to 4; A2 from 3 to 4; A2½ from 3 to 4: 32 oz. from 3 to 4: any other size or loose from 3 to 4 points per lb. (The 8 oz. and A1 cans remain at 2 and 3 points per can respectively.)
BISCUITS—MATZOS from 1 to 2 points per lb.
There will be no change in the value of coupons..
A=1, B=2, C=3, D=1, E=2.
DRIED EGGS: The allocation of Dried Eggs is now one packet per ration book every four weeks (as from April 29th); two for holders of green books.

Dill

FOOD FACTS

POTATO PETE says,
"*Now is the time to plant your herbs ; sage folk know they'll be worth a mint of money . . .*"

HERBS are good to eat, easy to grow. Year-round they'll put taste into your stews, soups, salads, savouries and sauces if you use them fresh or dried, according to season. Now is the time to plant them — in any sunny patch of earth or window-box. Some will even flourish in pots on an inside window sill (so long as it catches the sun) and pretty they'll look. All they ask of you is light, air and watering.

PARSLEY is perhaps the most important as it is rich in iron and in Vitamins A and C—a home-grown tonic in itself. But since it adds life to almost any dish—soup, salad, stew or savoury — to be self-supporting you need to grow quite a patch of it. Although it is an annual which you grow from seed, by sowing some now and more at the end of July, you can get an all-the-year-round crop.

NATIONAL WHEATMEAL BREAD

1. It is *more nourishing* than white bread;

2. It *keeps better*, tastes fresher;

3. It is rich in Vitamin B_1;

4. Most people report that it is the *nicest* bread they have ever eaten;

5. It *costs no more* than ordinary white bread.

Ask your Baker for National Wheatmeal Bread—and if he hasn't got it, *ask him again!* Although it is extra trouble for your Baker, he has promised the Ministry to supply National Wheatmeal Bread *if you order it.* It's up to you!

THE MINISTRY OF FOOD, LONDON, S.W.1

MINT also needs to be planted fairly generously to be worth cultivating. But if you can find the space —or even devote one whole window-box to it — the sweetness of the home-picked mint will repay you.

CHIVES chopped up in salads, soups or sandwiches taste just like spring onions. You use the tops instead of the tails so they go further than root onions.

CHIVES

THYME—both the lemon-flavoured and black varieties — are easy to grow and take up very little space (a pot of each will see most homes through).

SAGE for stuffing — yes, even without the onion (or *with* your chives) — a good strong taste for those who can take it. These are only a few of the many herbs which you can grow, and which you can buy as plants or seed for a few pence each.

AND NOW

Here are two dishes that are simply made by using mixed herbs (dried or fresh) :—

GREEN POTATOES are a good way of using up any boiled or steamed potatoes. Mash them up with a *nut of margarine*, a *teacupful of hot milk* or milk and water, salt and pepper and a pinch of sugar. Beat well with a fork and work in two good tablespoonfuls of chopped *mixed herbs* (whatever kinds you have — dried or fresh).

Or try Potato Soup this way. Chop up a few *chives* (the green part, remember) and cook them in a small *nut of margarine* until tender. Then scrub and dice up *two large raw potatoes* and put them in with the chives. Add a *teacupful* of *milk* and a *pint of water* and simmer gently until the potatoes are tender. Season with *salt and pepper* and add a dessert-spoonful of *flour-and-water paste* (to stop the potatoes from 'separating' and sticking to bottom of pan). Then throw in a teaspoonful of chopped *mixed herbs* for each plateful to be served.

Thyme   *Sage*

Aunt Gertrude's Chicken Tarragon

1 3½lb roasting chicken
1 garlic clove finely chopped
2 tbsps fresh tarragon chopped (if using dried tarragon 1 tbsp will be sufficient)
2 oz butter
juice of half-a-lemon
salt and freshly-ground black pepper
stock
3 tbsps brandy
extra butter for buttering outside of chicken

Wash the inside of chicken. Mix together the garlic, butter, tarragon and seasoning. Stuff this into the chicken. Now soften some more butter and rub this all over the chicken. Pour the lemon juice over the bird.

Put chicken in roasting pan and roast in a hot oven for 30 mins at 450°F. Then lower heat to 300°F and continue cooking for a further 40 mins, basting now and then with the butter. Now pour away some of the fat and mix the rest with ½ pint of stock (giblet stock is good). Heat this in a small saucepan to make a delicious gravy.

Slightly heat the brandy and pour it over the chicken. Set it alight. When the flames die down return the chicken to the oven for 10 mins. Then serve. This is a lovely party dish.

war-effort and, although there was a shortage of everything, we survived, and, indeed, were more healthy with our wartime food, in which dried eggs and margarine figured highly. Although the 1946–47 winter was the coldest for fifty-three years the holocaust was, after six years, over; and we were once more full of ideals for the Brave New World that we were about to build.

We raced on into the Fifties while the pace of life became faster and faster. Electricity opened up new ways to give us more leisure time in the home, which now began to be equipped with a washing-machine, refrigerator, dish washer, and many more gadgets to give women time off to resume their careers. Women's Lib was formed and the pattern of life changed once more. We began to recover somewhat from the agonising war-years. A new young queen came to the throne. There were spectacular athletic feats to thrill us every day. The way ahead was full of hope and expectation. Harold McMillan, the then Prime Minister, was reminding us

'You've never had it so good.' Enthusiasm was the keyword.

Aunt Gertrude did not live to see those stirring times. Her zest for life never left her and she kept on spreading happiness and hope until the end of her days. In the Forties she slept quietly away at nearly 100 years old. She had witnessed a completely changed world and her reaction to it was that of sympathy and understanding. Though her Herbal Lore goes on from strength to strength and is flourishing more strongly than ever, yet, somehow, the world grew a little colder, and a bit of magic vanished when Aunt Gertrude left us. And the garden doors 'letting out' the Peace and Happiness seemed to be closing all over the world. So that we have 'progressed' to violence, destruction and mob law. Maybe we should have a long look back to some of Aunt Gertrude's values of Yesterday and we might find a way to open the doors of Peace and Happiness once more.

Aunt Gertrude's Curative Ways with Nettles

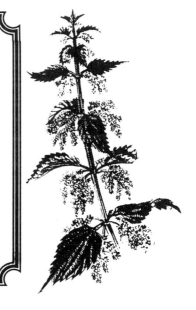

Young nettles cooked in butter like spinach make a delicious vegetable. They are invaluable as nutrients and curatives. They tone up the system and purify the blood. Aunt Gertrude used them a lot in this way.

She also made nettle tea. (A handful of nettles to a pint of boiling water. Infuse for 10 minutes. Sweeten with honey.) This is alkaline and a solvent of uric acid so it keeps rheumatism at bay. With its rich supply of iron it prevents anaemia.

She also made a nourishing and curative soup with nettles. It is delicious! Boil nettles, dandelion leaves and docks with a clove of garlic, sliced potatoes and a ham bone. Simmer for an hour and then strain. Serve very hot.

Give us a good digestion, Lord,
And also something to digest.
Give us a healthy body, Lord,
With sense to keep it at its best.

Give us a sense of humour, Lord,
Give us the grace to see a joke,
To get some happiness from life,
And pass it on to other folk.

Amen

129

Marjorie Watts

There are some topics which are always topical, and of these gardening comes top of the list for many people. That's one reason why the gardening spot on 'Day by Day' attracts a lot of attention. The other reason is the bubbling personality of our gardening expert, Marjorie Watts. Marjorie had the advantage of being born in the country, in Donemana, but didn't start to write and broadcast on the subject until the 1970s. Her enquiring mind came to the attention of the editor of the magazine 'Popular Gardening' and this led to a series of successful articles. It also brought Marjorie to the attention of the BBC and frequent broadcasts on programmes like 'Ulster Garden' soon followed. She claims that it was her son Alan, with the enquiring mind of a youngster, who helped train her for her subsequent 'career'. And now she passes on to me her own knowledge, though from time to time I appear to be not the brightest of pupils!

The Gardens of my Childhood

I have to laugh when people say, 'Were you always interested in gardening?' They think that I ran around with a wee spade digging and planting as soon as I could walk, but the truth is I never thought of such things until I was grown up and married. I had to start at the beginning then and learn my gardening the hard way, but I had two great things going for me – gardening parents and a country upbringing.

The lanes and meadows of my childhood were filled with flowers and if you move through a world of Clover and Purple Vetch, Stitchwort, Primroses, Speedwell and Ragged Robin it's bound to affect you, isn't it? We played in woods full of Bluebells and we knew where the Hazel Nuts grew and when to go looking for them. We used 'Docken' juice to soothe bare legs smarting from Nettle stings and we moved our fingers down the Foxtail Grass chanting 'Tinker, Tailor, Soldier, Sailor, Rich Man, Poor Man, Beggarman, Thief'. We took for granted Butterflies and Ladybirds and the strange Caterpillars we called 'Hairy Mollies'; We searched the meadows for acid-tasting Sorrel leaves while the Corncrakes called from fields where tractors and combine harvesters were unknown.

The first real garden to put a memory in my head for ever was my Grandmother's and I must have been very young then because I see it always in sunlight. I am alone there in the early morning and the world is huge and very still with dew sparkling on the grass and a fragrance of Cypress trees.

There's another picture in my mind from that time. Someone takes me through a door in a wall into a garden full of Apple and Pear trees with little low hedges all about and I feel a sense of wonder at this magic and secret place.

I have a distant memory of the garden at home, too, when I was about four years old. My mother is showing me a plant with grey leaves. 'Lamb's Ears,' she says and strokes it gently so that I may see how to touch a plant. 'Cups and Saucers,' she says, when we come to the Canterbury Bells. 'And here's a flower the same colour as your dress. It's called Love-in-a-Mist.'

But as we grew older, the garden played little part in our lives. What child would willingly share a world with adults when across the road and over the rusty gate, along the graveyard wall and through the 'Thistly field' was 'the Macaskey Burn'? Chuckling and amber and stony, it drew us along with it and took all sense of time away. Celandines grew there and Purple Loosestrife but the great golden flowers of the Marsh Marigolds seemed to me the most beautiful. Far away, in Belfast, where I had never been, other children made their memories and I smile to think of my husband as a little boy running with his brother through the fields at the back of the Lansdowne Road. Sometimes they earned pocket money by roaming around the suburban streets gathering sackfuls of material for their mother's compost heap. In a

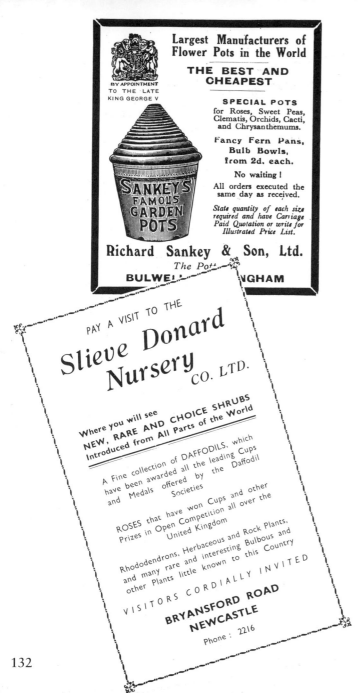
'bogey' made from old pram-wheels they collected the riches left by the horse-drawn traffic of those days. When they moved to Hawthornden Drive, there were fields behind the houses there too, and Jimmy remembers those fields being used as allotments during the 'Dig for Victory' campaign but in Macosquin we had always grown our own vegetables and my only war-time memory is of the garden gates being taken away for scrap iron.

Thinking back to my mother's store cupboards, fruit-growing must have played a big part in country gardens. I can see them now, those neatly-labelled jars of strawberry and raspberry jam, blackcurrant jelly, bramble and apple, gooseberry jam and rhubarb and ginger. There must have been a terrible punishment for children who dared take fruit from the bushes because I can't remember ever doing so. I can't remember many ornamental trees or shrubs from my childhood days either except that I was warned not to eat the yellow berries on a white Daphne bush, but such things were there, I'm sure. Sometimes I look through my mother's gardening catalogues dating from the Thirties and sigh for the plants that were lost when the specialist nurseries had to give way to the garden centres of today. But if garden centres bring more plants to the notice of more people then I don't regret them at all.

Grow for Winter
as well as Summer

DIG FOR VICTORY LEAFLET No. ... New Se...

Vegetables for you and your family every week of the year. Never a week without food from your garden or allotment. Not only fresh peas and lettuce in June— new potatoes in July, but all the health-giving vegetables in WINTER — when supplies are scarce - - - -

SAVOYS, SPROUTS, KALE, SPROUTING BROCCOLI, ONIONS, LEEKS, CARROTS, PARSNIPS and BEET

Vegetables all the year round
if you
DIG WELL
AND CROP WISELY

Follow this Plan ➡

ISSUED BY THE MINISTRY OF AGRICULTURE

With the introduction of food rationing, the Government were very keen to encourage people to make the most of their gardens.

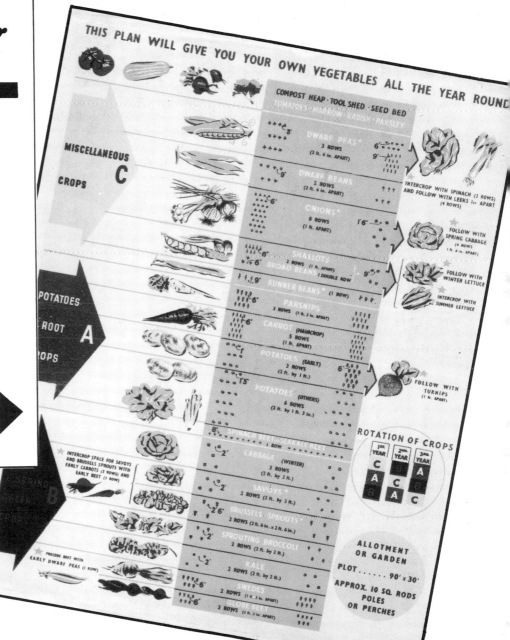

THIS PLAN WILL GIVE YOU YOUR OWN VEGETABLES ALL THE YEAR ROUND

SPECIAL GARDENING NUMBER.

People who appreciate gardens are not always those who like gardening. Nevertheless, to be a successful gardener you must have a real desire to grow things, just as to be a good cook it is necessary to enjoy cooking.

Of course, there are the favoured few for whom any twig or seed, casually planted, will root and multiply. Well-known also are the gardening manuals full of photographs of exhibition dahlias, and roses whose names read like a directory; full, too, of mysterious allusions to pruning, layering, and trenching It is possible, however, for almost anyone to gain a great deal of happiness from even a very small garden. It is better not to worry too much, but buy some packets of seed; beg or buy, and plant lavishly with both hands, a root here, a sprig there; get a reliable manure; air the earth round the roots with a fork

occasionally; keep a sharp look-out for slugs and wire-worms, and let the sun and the manure you have administered do the rest. Undoubtedly there is much more to be learnt, but the more difficult principles of gardening can be studied by degrees.

If your garden is not large it is a good idea to set aside one part for growing your raspberries, lettuces, and other dishes for the table, and decide on a special scheme for the rest. A competition might be run not only for the prettiest cottage garden, as one Institution is doing this summer, but for the most interesting rock-garden, the best-cared for vegetable plot, or well-stocked herb garden; or you might decide to concentrate on the sweet-smelling aromatic plants, bunches of which, dried, or made into pot-pourri, would be in great demand among your friends. Others might be more interested in making jams and pickles, and take many pains with their strawberry beds and cucumbers.

Unless you have a great deal of time, concentrating on one type of gardening and learning to master it thoroughly is by far the most satisfactory method of working. As you add to your particular collection of plants you find you grow more and more interested in them. They become personal and delightful friends. You will learn their likes and dislikes, and not only their names but their uses, some curious and superstitious, and something of their histories, which are closely bound up with the story of mankind, his experiments and adventures.

A garden, however small, provides a most satisfying pastime. It involves healthy, practical work, quantities of fresh air and good smells to dispel depression, and apart from producing good food and flowers, it has behind its beauty and usefulness a content which comes from the satisfaction of making things grow.

"The Countryman, sitting beside his cottage door, smoking an American weed in his pipe, while his wife shells the peas of ancient Rome into a basin, does not realise that his little garden, gay with Indian Pinks and African Geraniums, and all its small crowd of joyous-coloured flowers, is an open book of the history of his land spread at his feet. Here's the conquest of America, and the discovery of the Cape, and all the gold of Greece for his bees to play with. Here's his child making a chain of Chaucer's daisies; and there's a Chinese mandarin nodding at him from the Chrysanthemums; Lettuces from the Island of Cos, and Sir Walter Raleigh's Potato, the Cretan Quince, he Persian Peach, the Chinese Jessamine."
—From "The Charm of Gardens," D. C. Calthrop.

The picture on this page is from a lino-cut by Andy Cochrane, age 13, of Tullygrawley P.E. School, Cullybackey.

Of course there was also inspiration to be found in the Big Gardens. Trees and plants were often imported (at great difficulty and expense), like these ornamental bay trees which now grace the front of Mountstewart.

Memories come into your mind like coloured pictures, don't they? Looking back to the gardens of my childhood, the brightest picture of all, framed there for ever, is the Herbaceous Border. They were as common as rose beds are today and no-one ever complained that they were too much work or that they looked dreary in winter. I marvel now at all the staking and dividing and at the skilful way gardeners planted for 'progression' as they called it, with clumps of flowers coming into bloom from the beginning of the season until the autumn frosts. I can see those borders so clearly with their blue Delphiniums and pale pink Hollyhocks; Phlox and Carnations, Globe Flowers and Lupins; Michaelmas Daisies and pink Chrysanthemums and the Catmint spilling forward on to the path. Some of the plants were indestructible and you could see Paeonies, Solomon's Seal, Oriental Poppies and Christmas Roses still flourishing in old gardens when the hand that planted them had long since gone. 'Bedding plants' were unknown to us, but Canterbury Bells,

These postcards, produced for Woolworths by the NPO, were a novel way of marketing shamrock seed.

Prewar gardening magazines were full of interesting – and often lurid – advertisements.

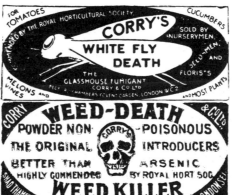

136

Forget-me-nots, Foxgloves, Sweet Williams, Brompton Stocks and Wallflowers mingled with Columbines and the 'Old Scotch Double Wallflower' called Harpur Crewe.

It's easy to be sentimental about such gardens, but what would the people who planted them think of the Heather and Conifer beds of today? Would they like our 'labour-saving shrubs', 'ground-cover plants', curved lines and patios? Would the 'Chemical Hoe' and the plastic urn fill them with envy or horror? I can't answer that, but if you are lucky enough to have an 'old-fashioned garden' then I think it must be a peaceful and pleasant place.

A good herbaceous border would make the summer riotous with colour as this Belfast garden shows.

137

ACKNOWLEDGEMENTS

I'm sure it is no exaggeration to describe this book as a labour of love by all those who contributed to it. But it would not have been possible to complete it without the kind and willing help of a number of people. Among them are Mr John Killen and the staff of the Linen Hall Library; the staff of the Belfast Central Library; the Federation of Women's Institutes, and in particular Mrs Mary Boyd of Kilrea W.I. and a former Chairman of the Federation; the staff of the *County Down Spectator*; Robert Agnew of the Grand Opera House; Ms Judy Maxwell of Downpatrick Race Course; Mr D.S. Kewley of the Reading Centre at Stranmillis College; Ms Sally Kelso; and Mr John Minnion who was responsible for the pictorial representation of me on p.13, which first appeared in the pages of *Radio Times*. I would like to thank my good friend Rowel Friers (and The Blackstaff Press) for permission to reproduce the cartoon from his forthcoming book, *On The Borderline*, which appears on p.20; Bill Nesbitt and The Blackstaff Press for the poem 'The Big Day Out', from *The Only Place For Me*; the *Tyrone Constitution* for the poems from Matt Mulcahy's *The Rhymes of a Besom Man* on pp.6, 68, 83; and the many individuals and organisations who gave permission to use the photographs and other illustrative material which appear throughout the book; the BBC (pp.vi, 4, 5, 6, 8, 9, 10, 17, 50) and the BBC Hulton Picture Library (pp.16, 18); the *Belfast News Letter* (p.60); the *Belfast Telegraph* (pp.2, 54, 55, 58, 62, 67); the Deputy Keeper of the Records of Northern Ireland (p.43); the National Trust (p.135); *Woman's Own* (p.98); Dr G.H.S. Boyd of Stranmillis College (p.109); the proprietors of Dunmore Stadium (p.59); Mrs Pearl Dunning (p.94); Mrs P. Whan (p.122); Mr Sydney Smith (p.115); Mrs Nora Murphy (p.112); Mrs William Brownlow (p.105); Mrs A. Elliot (p.137); Carey McClay of the Northern Publishing Office (p.136); Messrs Robinson & Cleaver and Anderson & McAuley for the numerous advertisements they allowed us to reproduce; and last but not least The Ulster Folk and Transport Museum who let us reproduce some of their collection of wartime ephemera.

I always like to thank the contributors to the programme individually for their contributions. It is a particular pleasure to thank all of them collectively for their contributions to this book (and for the many illustrations they unearthed for us).